ADVEN DAYZE

Overcoming Fears and Limitations to Trek Britain and Ireland's Highest Points

WAYNE MULLANE

Disclaimer

Please note: before undertaking any new exercise or dieting plan, you should always consult your physician, especially if you have any pre-existing medical or physical conditions. If it begins to hurt, stop – preventing injury is better than trying to break your personal best for exercise, whether it be press-ups or hiking up a mountain. I am not a doctor of any kind, therefore I am unable to offer advice from a professional point of view; I'm just letting you know what works for me personally.

Dedicated to all my family and friends –
thank you for sharing this journey of life

Table of Contents

Introduction 1

Section One: Background **6**

Chapter One: The Backstory 7

Chapter Two: Preparation 16

Chapter Three: Fitness 20

Section Two: The Walks **27**

Chapter Four: First Walk of Winter 28

Chapter Five: The London One 37

Chapter Six: The Beast From The East Knocks Us Off Our Feet 45

Chapter Seven: Shame: Rain Again! 53

Chapter Eight: Beacon Hill Bonanza 61

Chapter Nine: Will the Real Walbury Hill Please Stand Up? 69

Chapter Ten: Hungry Hikers 77

Chapter Eleven: The Big Weekend 83

Chapter Twelve: 2019 Walks 101

Chapter Thirteen: 2020 Part One 121

Chapter Fourteen: 2020 Part 2 139

Chapter Fifteen: 2020 Part 3 154

Section Three: Advice and Guidance **162**

Chapter Sixteen: Why I Walk 163

Chapter Seventeen: Kit List and Staying Safe 168

Chapter Eighteen: Dealing with Heights 178

Chapter Nineteen: Technology 185

Chapter Twenty: How to Choose A Walk 188

Conclusion 191

Appendix 192

Acknowledgements 202

Introduction

Ben Nevis. Big old Ben Nevis. It's there, it's big, and it deserves respect.

Situated in the Grampian Mountains of West Scotland, at 1345 metres high Ben Nevis is the tallest mountain in the UK.

Thousands of people climb or hike this mountain every year, and in 2018 it became the ultimate British walking destination for me and three of my friends (Aaron, Robert, and Robin). Having focused on the tallest mountains in England and Wales in 2016 and 2017 respectively, we then turned our attention to 'the mountain with its head in the clouds'.

We knew that having a yearly focal point for our exercising endeavours would help us achieve our goals and encourage us to persevere with our hiking – something that is very important considering how many advantages come with walking.

Yes, walking has a number of benefits, for both mental health (such as reducing stress and anxiety) and physical health (such as maintaining a healthy weight and preventing conditions like heart disease and diabetes). It is a low-impact form of exercise, and it needn't involve much more than putting on a pair of trainers and popping outside for a while. Then, if you enjoy it and want to start exploring beyond your own locality, there are seemingly endless places in which you can create your own escapades.

Walking is a flexible activity that can either be enjoyed alone or with family or friends, and – more importantly – it isn't a hobby that has to break the bank; keep it low-cost by staying local and taking some sarnies and a drink with you, or save up and go on days out further afield. You can do it in an hour, a day, or longer. Whether you follow pre-planned routes from websites, create your own, or join a walking group, there's also enormous fun to be found in the planning and anticipation of your stroll or hike.

The journeys you take will, no doubt, be well worth remembering, and that is part of the reason why I wrote this book: it's great to have something to look back on, and recording what I've achieved has given me a true sense of enjoyment that only increases every time I head outdoors. Now, I want to pass on this sense of enjoyment to you.

The first section of this book looks at my backstory, including how my friends and I organised our holiday to Scotland along with our other fitness pursuits. The second part examines selected treks undertaken by myself and my friend Robin, including the issues we had to face – and the obstacles we had to overcome – before our big weekend away in Scotland with our friends. I then look at my walking pursuits of 2019, including how we took on the highest mountain in the Republic of Ireland and how I made good progression in combatting my acrophobia (fear of heights).

Originally, I was hoping to self-publish this book in the spring of 2020, but then the Coronavirus pandemic rocked both the world and my writing. However, during this time I was able to develop some novel ways in which to continue hiking while also tackling my altitude anxieties, which I'll share with you in that section.

In the final section of the book, I offer my experience and knowledge to those considering taking up walking as a hobby; chapters in this section cover why I walk, dealing with heights, technology, building up a hiking kit, and staying safe.

This is not simply a guidebook, and nor is it a full account of every single walk I've ever done; it's somewhere in between. I wanted to show you how hiking has changed my mindset, my perspective, and my health – and how it can do the same for you. Similarly, this book isn't an account of my whole life but more my hiking life, with certain memories sprinkled in for good measure; I wanted to show you that hiking – and even writing about hiking – has the power to evoke wonderful feelings and events of one's past. (If you'd like to know more about my other work and interests, you can find my website and email address at the back of the book.)

Whether you're brand new to hiking – perhaps because you're getting out more on foot during times of lockdown – or a seasoned rambler, it's my hope that this book will encourage you to keep on exploring and creating your own adventures. You'll see that, despite my best efforts to plan and execute our journeys with a calm and organised state of mind, one characteristic flaw or another always inevitably pops up – hence why this book is called Adventure Dayze. I'm nearly always in a daze on days out, leaving me in a complete spin about what to do, with my acrophobia constantly challenging me as well.

Over time, I've learnt not to let my preconceptions, doubts, or a befuddled brain keep me from my travels (although there are definitely times when I know I need to respect my limitations), as such things can only add to the memory of any outing and, thankfully, my mates are always on hand to keep me sane – at least long enough for us to achieve our shared goal!

In some of these chapters I've included a 'handy tips' section, and you can also find all of these tips in the book's Appendix, collected together for your convenience. Also in the Appendix you'll find a list of resources to help you in your walking endeavours, including websites and apps I use on a regular basis.

As I've said, this book is not a guidebook for particular hikes; it is more an overview of hiking and its benefits, as well as the story of my own journey with walking as I overcome limitations and conquer my fears in order to become a fully-fledged hiker with a great love of the outdoors.

As many of the walks were planned through Google Maps and then subsequently un-planned as we spontaneously chose different tracks, I am unable to provide links to the walks we actually did – and that's kind of the point of this book. I want to encourage people to get out there and start walking, whether they can read print maps or not. Walking is all about venturing out in the fresh air, getting moving, and enjoying the wonderful countryside. You can plan it meticulously if you want, and you should always be sensible when you're out and about, but I find the real magic is in discovering the unknown and carving your own path.

Hikes provide the chance to fulfil many kinds of interests: history, geography, nature, photography, and physical and mental well-being, just to name a few. I could have gone into the historical aspects relating to a number of walks in this book, but as I began writing it became clear that there were other themes I needed to explore more (such as heights, friendship, getting lost, food, and fitness).

Hiking may take a lot of organisation – and you may come across many obstacles along the way – but in my opinion, it's always worth it. And, as with anything in life, it's not necessarily about the destination; it's about the journey you take to get there, and the wonderful things you see and experience along the way.

Please note that this book was due for publication in Spring 2020, before the Coronavirus Pandemic hit and the way we hiked – and did everything – changed. In the 2018 and 2019 sections I mention taking public transport and visiting pubs as part of the hiking experience. I decided to keep these chapters in their original form, despite the changes brought on by the pandemic, as a reminder of more regular times that were and that are to come again. However, at the time of writing this introduction (February 2021), it's fair to say that the government guidelines around visiting hospitality venues and taking public transport have been subject to much change in the past year. The day will come where, yet again, we'll be able to freely sit in a beer garden or jump on a train to wherever we like. Until such a time, please adhere to the government's Covid-19 guidance when planning a hike (www.gov.uk).

SECTION ONE:

BACKGROUND

Chapter One

THE BACKSTORY

My three mountain-walking mates and I have known each other since our A-level days, back in the early nineties, when we were all growing up in the industrial town of Slough in South East England. Even though the countryside framed our hometown on all sides, at the time we didn't really appreciate how close we were to a right rural adventure. At that age, you don't, do you?

Well, time moved on, and – with the exception of Aaron, who now lives in Yorkshire – the rest of us settled down in different parts of Berkshire, with me personally moving to Maidenhead. These days we're four early forty-somethings, all reasonably content with life. In recent years, however, we've found ourselves wanting more, wanting something else…wanting a change. We needed to do something different, something to take us out of our comfort zones and beyond the normal routines of our day-to-day lives.

Back in May 2016, Robin and I started our rural outings – just around our county and surrounding counties – as a means of having something to do at the weekends and to keep ourselves fit. Soon, it became clear that the fresh air and open spaces gave us the chance to gain a soul-cleansing, fresh perspective on life, something that very much added to its appeal. Once we realised this, we decided to make it a regular thing.

This really is the true joy of walking. The fresh air is good for your body, but it's also so important for your mind – as is the simple act of getting your body moving, which resets the mind and helps you look at things from a different point of view. Exercise (especially when done outdoors) has so many benefits for your physical and mental health, and many people have started using it more as a means to help with their own self-development than as a means of increasing their fitness – the fitness is just an added benefit. Movement equals mind health, and walking gives you a real sense of worth. Plus, the countryside is uncomplicated – unlike built-up and overrun towns and cities – and being in such lavish natural surroundings does so much to calm the mind. I find it's necessary to stop and sit at least once on a hike simply to revel in the beauty of where I'm at – that alone imbues me with a sense of peace and stops me feeling overwhelmed.

When Robin and I first started walking, we'd barely manage six or seven miles – and that was only if we took short breaks every so often. Within a few weeks, though, we were notching up 10 miles at a time, only breaking once for lunch. We joined a local walking group, but found that we'd much rather do our own trips as we enjoyed the element of spontaneity in following our own treks and the sense of freedom and discovery that brought with it. Plus, doing our own thing gave us the chance for some quiet introspection, and to recharge from this fast-paced world.

So, during the working week Robin and I would email back and forth, sending each other routes we'd either found on websites or created ourselves using Google Maps. There was only one rule: there had to be a pub en route for a lunch stop. I loved plotting these routes, and the planning of our hikes became a really enjoyable part of the whole process; it added several layers of anticipation as we looked forward to discovering all these new places once the weekend rolled around.

One weekend in June, Aaron popped down to see us all, and – as we sat together in a Reading pub – Robin and I embarked on an enthusiastic discourse about our new hobby while Aaron and Robert listened intently. As the conversation flowed, the idea of tackling the highest peaks in each country of the British Isles was brought up.

England's highest peak of Scafell Pike would be first on the list – I can't remember who came up with this idea exactly, as my mind was rather blurred after a few pints – and it was decided that we'd tackle this at the end of July. Snowdon and then Ben Nevis would follow, over the next two summers. We did (briefly) consider doing the famous 24-hour Three Peaks Challenge, but this was quickly discarded. Doing one peak a year would give us a focal point for us to meet up as a foursome every 12 months. Besides, back then, the Three Peaks Challenge would probably have been beyond me, fitness-wise.

Over our pints, we all made the decision to accept this self-imposed challenge, agreeing to up our health regimes in the meantime. Aaron and Robert were already keen runners and would carry on in that way, whereas Robin and I committed to our countryside patrols with added vim. The beauty of walking is that we knew we didn't have to become fixated on developing rippling muscles to achieve our hiking goals; in fact, my slightly wobbly belly is a reminder to me of the importance of finding a good pub during a trek.

In preparation, I watched several YouTube videos on Scafell Pike, read up on what to take, and spoke to friends who'd already conquered the mountain.

So, when we started our ascent of the Pike, I mentally applauded myself for doing my homework and for the commitment I'd made to making sure this momentous day went smoothly.

A third of the way up the 987-metre rise, I paused briefly to enjoy the beautiful views of rugged scenery and streams cascading through the hills, and when I properly stopped to look at the world around us, I became mesmerised by everything the Lake District had to offer.

Some of Aaron's friends from Yorkshire had joined us and we all chatted jovially as we made our way up. I was having a great time, enjoying the fresh air, the exercise, and the feeling of accomplishment that was washing over me the nearer we got to the top.

Something, however, was about to change all that.

I went through an instant personality change about half-way up when I was visited by my arch-enemy: a certain FEAR OF HEIGHTS. All of a sudden the gradient became far steeper, and my legs stopped working as I started panicking about the distance and gradient ahead. In an instant my head began to swim and I became less sure-footed.

Why hadn't it occurred to me that climbing up this mountain would involve being at altitude?

My body slowed down as I began to assess every step in great detail, and for the rest of the day I trailed behind the group, just trying to keep it together. It was absurd of me not to have considered the altitude factor, especially considering how many YouTube videos I'd watched in preparation.

In my blissful ignorance, I'd completely underestimated the challenge and how it would affect me – both physically and mentally.

My mates were great, willing me on and encouraging me every time I slowed down too much, but that didn't stop me from cussing myself. I felt bitter and irritated; all I wanted to do was enjoy the landscape, enjoy the time with my friends, and accomplish the challenge with vigour, yet I was impeded from doing so because all I could think about was my own survival. From here on in, my memory of the scenery became so patchy that I could only give a loose, basic description of what I observed – rocky outcrops, streams, steep hills, and scree fields all featured at some point, I know that much – as I was far more concerned about plummeting down the side of the mountain.

The last 150 metres or so became very rocky and, with my fading state of mind, I started worrying about getting to the top.

Coming to a halt, I told my friends that I'd stay where I was, and that I'd wait for them to reach the peak – they could then join me again as they came back down. Robert, Robin, and Aaron persevered with me, however, and I appreciated them dropping off the pace to support me as we all headed to the peak – no man left behind.

Footstep by footstep, as my inward cussing turned to complete self-loathing, we made our way to the top. We were so close, but just before we got there I stumbled, nearly getting my foot wedged between two rocks. Yet, somehow – and despite everything – I made it.

Amongst the low temperature, swirling mists, and other mountain-goers, there I stood with my friends at the cairn that marked the summit. We'd done it.

The rest of the group wandered about the rocky top, investigating a disused building and some other dilapidated structures, as well as turning full circle to obtain views of the beautiful scenery from all angles. I, however, wasn't being quite so exploratory; I sat a few metres away from the cairn, munching on a pasty and trying to gear myself up for the way back down.

Indeed, this was just a brief respite before tackling the descent: the return leg would find me reliving all my previous feelings – but this time with the added worry (and nausea) of possibly tumbling down a steep slope. One…step…at…a…time.

My friends kept pace with me, distracting themselves with Pokémon GO while I feared for my life, though I paused long enough to stare in awe as we passed a barefooted bloke making his way up the slopes. Then, as we crossed a stream and I filled my water bottle, Aaron was kind enough to remind me that I could be drinking diluted sheep's wee!

Soon, the descent became more bearable and I was finally able to enjoy my surroundings again. Gradually, I became more and more relaxed, and once I was sure I wouldn't go tumbling to my death, I thanked my mates for their support and encouragement.

When we finally reached the valley floor, I could have dropped to my knees and kissed the ground; instead, I thanked God for helping me get through this testing ordeal.

When talk of doing Snowdon in the summer of 2017 started up again, I thought of my experience up Scafell Pike and immediately ruled myself out. So, when I found myself on a frosty January morning in 2017 traipsing the Oxfordshire-Berkshire border between Goring and Pangbourne in preparation for Wales' tallest peak, I had to laugh. I was doing this against my best instincts, and to top it off I looked like the world's worst ice skater as I slid over the black ice on those cold country lanes.

If I was going to do this, I told myself, I would put myself through whatever I needed to do in order to improve from my experience on Scafell Pike, albeit within reason: I knew, for instance, that I couldn't commit to running or attending the gym regularly as I'm too self-conscious when exercising in front of other people, and gyms can be expensive. Also, I live in the in-between phase of the couch potato and moderate fitness fan. So, doing occasional workouts at home, along with a steady amount of walking, would provide enough stimulus to get me fighting fit for the challenge (this approach actually laid the blueprint for my fitness goals when I was training for Ben Nevis – see chapter three).

Robin committed to a lot of solo weekday walks, and then we'd both meet on alternate weekends to put some more miles in together. The apex of our training was when we went on a weekend break in the Pewsey Vale in Wiltshire, which culminated in us conquering the highest point in the county – Milk Hill, which stands at 297 metres – as part of a 17-mile hike.

Aaron and Robert ran and ran. And when they finished running, they ran some more.

Again, I spent plenty of time checking various websites and watching YouTube videos on how to prepare for Snowdon, and it seemed that the tourist path we were going to take was a well laid-out route. I had repeated concerns about drops and descending mists, but chats with friends who'd been to the roof of Wales assured me this would be a much better endeavour than Scafell Pike.

Fortunately, they were right. The tourist path – also known as the Llanberis Path – is often referred to as 'The Motorway' due to the sheer number of people who use it. Even with a constant drizzle on the ascent and a heavy fog that greeted us about two-thirds of the way up, this journey was truly uplifting – if a bit of a slog in parts. At least here it was easier to stop and enjoy the breathtaking views of the far-below valleys and remote farmsteads, if just for a few moments.

As time went on I became more and more aware that I was feeling less wary about the height, mainly as I had a clear, wide path in front of me. Plus, there was a café halfway up, and one at the top, both of which acted as safe havens for me, allowing me to take a rest and psyche myself up for the remainder of the course.

Despite my fears, the feelings I'd had on Scafell Pike didn't surface on Snowdon at all – save for a slight bit of anxiety – and soon we'd reached the peak and had headed back down again.

You may ask why, when I'm advocating the mental health benefits of walking, I would write about myself being a quivering wreck while traipsing up a mountain. All I can say is that, despite having a certain fear of heights, I love being at altitude; the benefits to my mental health of being high up far outweigh my level of acrophobia. So, it was after the Snowdon trip that I rationalised my behaviour, knowing that if I wanted to experience the joy of being in high-up places, I'd need to endure my acrophobia. I'd need to push myself through my mental distress in order to break through and experience true joy.

After we'd finished our Welsh odyssey, discussion turned to Ben Nevis. Right away, I said I was up for it – with the proviso that, as it was around 250m higher than Snowdon, I might not make it all the way. This, of course, was my fear of heights talking again, but my friends reassured me that I should simply do whatever I could.

I just hoped it wouldn't be as bad as Scafell Pike.

Chapter Two

PREPARATION

'We need to move quickly, then,' pondered Aaron, 'to avoid a repeat of last year.'

'Sure, having a good place to stay is a must,' I replied. 'The trouble is, everywhere within our price range seems to be booked up already.'

It was late January 2018 and we'd encountered an issue with finding somewhere to stay in Scotland. On our previous trips to Scafell Pike and Snowdon we'd simply camped: low budget, no thrills. However, the few days away at Snowdon had been blighted by high winds and driven rain that had seen tents blown over and flooded. We certainly didn't want a repeat of that.

As with previous years, we'd initially all thought it would be no problem to find anywhere with a few months to go, but Robin had a hunch matters would be different this time. Following this, I'd phoned around one afternoon to try and get us a place, and after speaking to a man at a bothy near Fort William, I'd been fair warned that the more affordable accommodation for late spring and early summer can go early in the New Year.

I relayed this to Aaron on the phone that evening.

'I'll set about putting up some date choices. We need to stress to the others that we have to start moving on this,' proffered Aaron.

'I agree. I'll keep searching for accommodation. Maybe the two Robs will have an idea too.'

For the Snowdon trip, Aaron had found a date-scheduling website that enabled the four of us to select from a range of dates. This cut the need to be endlessly contacting each other or to be trawling back through WhatsApp messages to see what had or hadn't been agreed on, which would inevitably throw us into an interminable loop of trip organising. For more information on the resources we used to organise our trip, check out the Useful Resources section in the Appendix.

To begin with, Aaron chose a date range of May to July for Ben Nevis. The problem with being blokes, though, is that at some point we're going to get distracted by things like watching TV and other important stuff – such as doing nothing in particular. In the ensuing weeks, therefore, there'd been an odd flicker of conversation about holiday dates, without anything solid being put in place. Then, on the last Saturday of February, during a day out in London (see chapter six), Robin brought up the subject of accommodation once again.

'I've found us somewhere to stay on Airbnb,' he began, 'depending on what dates we agree on.'

'What sort of place is it?' I enquired.

'A holiday home in Fort William,' he beamed. 'Right in the main town.'

It struck me there and then that this would mean a bed each, a private bathroom, TV…things camping definitely couldn't offer us. We'd not become anti-camping exactly – the events of Snowdon hadn't put us off entirely – but the lure of having a more luxurious base for our Scottish adventure appealed to each and every one of us the second it was mentioned.

Having a place completely to ourselves also meant that we wouldn't be restricted by normal hotel or BnB rules. Now, we were gloriously free to freak out to heavy rock music at 3am, if we so chose.

A week later, everything was set for a weekend in early June. Robin had also found a decent deal on flights for him, Robert and myself; Aaron would drive up from Yorkshire and collect the rest of us from Glasgow Airport before taking us to Fort William (the nearest town to Ben Nevis).

I was relieved that everything was finally sorted. As I'm sure you know, organising a weekend away – or any kind of holiday – is something worth celebrating in itself: it's one of life's mini victories. While we're on the topic, eating a pork pie or scotch egg in any place at any time count as mini victories too. Go on: have a meat or vegetarian scotch egg with ketchup (optional) right now and you'll see what I mean. Actually, the ketchup isn't optional, it's compulsory. (That's a good hiking tip right there: always take a few sachets of tomato sauce with you. You never know when you might need it!)

We were so elated that we'd finally booked our holiday; the only thing that could hold us back now would be somebody stealing Ben Nevis itself.

Chapter Three

FITNESS

Before I took up hiking as a hobby, most evenings saw me pitched up in front of the TV, stuffing my face with snacks. Consequently, over the period of a few years, my belly had felt like a slowly inflating rubber ring. I knew I needed to shed a few pounds and stop myself from becoming near comatose after work every day, but dieting has always felt far too regimented to me – and, besides, I like the idea of being free to eat a pie if I want to. That left exercise as my only option.

Going out for a run or to the gym didn't appeal as – like I've said – I'd become too self-conscious of exercising in front of other people. Walking, however, gave me the impetus to exercise at my own pace and in my own way; it could be done fast or slow, and over any distance I wanted. Plus, it allowed me to be out and about, exercising in the fresh air while not having to experience the pressures of looking like a flapping fish being reeled in by an angler – which is exactly what my running style looks like.

Yes, walking suited me down to the ground. A tight exercise regime or healthy lifestyle may be necessary for some, but personally, I needed to switch off once in a while, and – more importantly – eat cake guilt-free.

During 2016 and 2017, all I did was walk (with the addition of the occasional workout for Snowdon); short distances of a few miles once or twice a week were followed by six to 10 miles with Robin on alternating weekends. At this stage, Robin had a similar approach to me, and – by the time we did Snowdon in 2017 – this approach had definitely seen us through.

However, we believed Ben Nevis needed a little something extra. Yes, we'd managed to build up ongoing levels of fitness, but now we were going higher than we'd ever been before, and we knew we needed to respect the challenge by being a little more devoted to our health goals. When we'd been preparing for Scafell Pike, Aaron had told me that if we were able to walk the equivalent of the ascent and descent on flat ground on a regular enough basis, we'd be fine. As the total round trip for Ben Nevis is about eight miles, that wouldn't be a problem – and there'd be no harm in gaining that extra fitness to help sustain us in our undertaking.

So, by the start of 2018, Robin had hit the gym whilst Aaron and Robert remained committed to their jogging regime. I found myself in a state of ambiguity: on the one hand I wanted to exercise, but on the other I wasn't sure how or where. Robin had given me a pep talk about going to the gym, saying that the best way to face my fear was simply to go there, but I wasn't so sure. I put it off, then put it off some more.

With Robin's words going round and round in my mind, I spent some time examining precisely why gyms and jogging didn't cut it for me, and I came to the conclusion that it was precisely a case of others judging me. The guys constantly told me not to worry about that and to focus on myself, but I just couldn't help it – which was particularly strange as we all used to go jogging when we lived in Slough. Similarly, if I took up a team sport, that would open my mind to being compared to teammates. I thought it was stupid for somebody my age to be so self-conscious – especially as it's only ever to do with sport – and while it's not exactly an overwhelming sensation, it's simply how I am.

I'd always thought that, as I aged, I'd become less inhibited about doing what I wanted to do, but that just didn't seem to be the case. This was particularly strange as walking up mountains was, in part, about me challenging my fear of heights; why couldn't I also challenge this dread I had concerning exercising in public?

Maybe this was exactly what it was: an age-related, self-contained, contradictory point of view. Or maybe, I pondered further, it was simply because these forms of exercise didn't appeal to me. If you tell me I have to run a quarter of a mile, I'll shut down; if you tell me I have to walk 15 miles, before you can say 'physical exercise' my boots will be on and I'll be out the door.

So, I found myself in a quandary. As Robert and Aaron pounded the streets and parks and as Robin pumped iron down at the gym, the lure of the sofa became attractive once again, particularly as January 2018 wore on. Regular walking had slowed down due to the colder weather, and although I toyed with the idea of buying weights and doing sit-ups and press-ups at home, the idea really didn't appeal.

No, I needed something else. I needed something low budget and enjoyable. Something I wanted to do and would *actually* do.

It took me the best part of January to find a solution, and I can't remember how or why I first decided to do it, but I started working out my own fitness programme. I borrowed a few ideas from exercise videos on YouTube, and soon I had my own regime in place that I could mix up with about fifteen or so different exercises to choose from. Plus, it was free (if you ignored my monthly broadband payment).

I started small: 15 or 20 minutes at first, building up to no more than thirty minutes at a time. Then, as the weeks went by, I added new types of exercises and took others away, eventually buying a pair of ankle weights to boost my efforts. I used my home to suit my regime: I gripped the tops of door frames to stretch out; I did standing press-ups against the kitchen worktops; and I pranced around the living room like an uncoordinated starfish as I stepped and jumped about.

As the routines varied in duration, I could quite happily complete a five or 10-minute workout some evenings and be happy with that – the important thing was that I remained committed.

Finally, I'd found an answer that didn't involve being in close proximity to judging eyes as I worked up a sweat.

Roughly around the same time, Robin and I began to diet. Since hitting forty, I'd grown more outward than upwards, and now seemed as good a time as any to tackle that. Although, as I've said, I find it hard being restricted to tight regimens, which inevitably led me to start snacking heavily again. As February turned into March – and with our walking time being restricted by heavy downpours of snow – a new lean, mean Robin had put himself out there, whilst a fitter-slightly-less-fatter Wayne was now on display.

I was still battling between all-out exercise and all-out eating, living some kind of half-existence as I tried to satisfy two extremes. For all the crisps, sandwiches, and chocolate I ate, I'd attempt to make up for it by doing an ultra-workout, but soon my body started telling me I was overdoing it. I'd leave longer gaps between workouts, even though I knew my efforts were at risk of coming undone.

I didn't want to give up exercising, though. I really enjoyed following exercise videos on YouTube and then incorporating them into my own routines; it engaged both my brain and my body, in all sorts of ways. Regular exercise is well known to boost mood and I was keen to benefit from that.

Robin, Robert, and Aaron had kept on exercising, battling their own fitness demons, and I knew I needed an extra incentive to get me through – at least until the snow cleared and I could commit to regular distance walking again.

'It's all about your mindset, you know,' Robert told me one evening as he supped his pint.

'Okay,' I replied, a little uncertainly. I'd explained my predicament to him over after-work drinks as we waited for Robin to join us one early March evening. We were in Reading again – we spend a lot of time there.

'Yeah,' Robert replied. 'You feel guilty for eating more food, so you punish yourself with full-on exercise.'

'Go on,' I encouraged him.

'Eventually, you give up, because you find that trying to satisfy two complete opposites just doesn't work,' he continued with a nod.

'So what do I do?'

'Like I said, change your mindset. You like exercising, and you also like snacks, yeah? So, exercise to snack.'

'Exercise to snack,' I repeated, and a moment of clarity engulfed me. As I said this over and over again in my mind, a smile began to form on my face. I could force myself through gruelling workouts with the promise of a pork pie or a fondant fancy at the end – and feel guilt-free to boot!

'Snackercise!' I exclaimed happily.

'Exactly. Just accept that what you're already doing is okay and you'll be fine. You'll lose weight more slowly, but that doesn't matter – so long as you're okay with it.'

I was certainly okay with it; in fact, I celebrated my redefined moderately healthy lifestyle with a swig of my highly calorific pint. Really, I wouldn't be doing anything different – I'd just have a fresh approach to motivate me. Plus, having a target like Ben Nevis to focus on gave me extra incentive to keep working out. Sure, the pounds didn't exactly drop off, but I definitely became fitter as I occasionally increased my workouts each week to supplement all the walking.

It really is amazing how just a few simple words gave me that much-needed clarity while forcing away the indecisiveness that had been holding me back. Mindset certainly is a powerful thing.

So, by the time the Ben Nevis weekend rolled around, I might have been a few pounds heavier than I'd planned at the start of the year, but I was fitter than I'd felt in years and more than ready for the challenge.

Handy Tips

Pop along to YouTube and tap 'workout videos' into the search bar. Change it up by putting in 'five-minute workouts' or '10-minute workouts', or just walk! Walking carries a myriad of benefits for both physical and mental health (see the chapter 'Why I Walk' for more information on how it's helped me).

Section Two:

THE WALKS

Chapter Four

FIRST WALK OF WINTER

After an extended hiatus following Christmas and New Year, Robin and I resumed our walking duties on the first Saturday of February 2018. The four-month road to Ben Nevis started here.

We met at Reading train station, ready for what should have been an easy seven-mile round loop encompassing town and country, which I'd planned out beforehand using Google Maps. As constant drizzle spattered our faces, we left the urban sprawl behind us and soon we were hugging the River Thames as we traversed west through the long country lane to the village of Mapledurham, which was to be our halfway turnaround point. The chance to be far away from crowds of people certainly is an enticing aspect of country walks, especially for a semi-introvert-ed soul like me.

However, drizzle soon turned to rain, and ahead, the foot-path had softened to such an extent that at times I slipped and twisted through the mud, having to hold on to branches to steady myself as I went. Robin was a lot more sure-footed than I was, and whenever I looked up he'd always be a good 20 metres ahead – a reminder to me that I'd need to be a lot more solid on my pins if I was going to have any chance of negotiating the hostile terrain of the Ben.

This first outing of the year was meant to be a stroll past farm fields in order to gently build up our fitness. However, at a fork in the path we saw a hill to our right, and in instantaneous agreement we decided to change tack and venture out on a new route. Leaving the views of the Thames behind us, we got ready to work those muscles.

This first hill was suitable for starters: a smooth, flat road that rose gently between farm fields. At one stage we had to keep our wits about us as we passed a paintball centre; suddenly the constant downpour seemed far more welcoming than a face full of paint from someone's rogue shot.

As we reached the top of the climb, we checked the maps on our phones to see there was a pub about a mile and a half up the road, heading east. Like all good walks, ours was about to go seriously off course in the search of good ale.

Soon, as the fields gave way to costly homes with sweeping driveways, the solitude of the path was replaced by the threat of being run over or splashed by passing vehicles along a B-road. We hurried along until we turned onto the road with the pub.

This was the main country road heading out of Reading towards Oxford, and I should have had my senses about me as I calmly plodded out into oncoming traffic, only to be pulled back by Robin.

Stepping out of the rainstorm and into the pub was like being welcomed into heaven: we were warm, safe, and dry, among other walkers and families in a bar that gave off the air of being a country cottage, complete with roaring fire blazing invitingly in the corner. Refusing to succumb to my food demons, I settled for quiche and salad rather than the usual offering of burger and fries, while Robin opted for pasta. Willing each other on in terms of fitness and diet would be essential for the months ahead – although, as you know, the whole diet thing never lasts long with me.

'We can't let winter beat us,' Robin began, during chompings.

'It won't,' I replied confidently. 'I'm working out, you've hit the gym…'

'But what if we hit bad weather for walks?'

'Well, we have about sixteen weeks left; if we continue meeting every fortnight like we do, that gives us about eight long walks to practice.'

'Yeah, but we need a back-up plan if the winter weather gets really shoddy. Blizzards aside, nothing should stop us,' said Robin.

'Hmmm,' I pondered.

The inclement and boggy conditions of this footslog – as well as the potential for winter snow falling at any time – had now caused us to rethink our preparations. For the two previous mountain trainings we'd called walks off in revolting weather; now, though, the energy and the level of commitment had become far more palpable in our ambitions to conquer Mr Nevis.

'Well, being out in this is good practice if conditions become arduous in Scotland,' I said, not able to offer anything more.

'I just get this feeling that the weather is going to be more against us than in previous years,' warned Robin.

When Robin has thoughts like this it's worth taking note, because oftentimes his hunches prove right. Now, with no immediate answer, we suspended making our decision and instead turned our attention to the day's football news.

We rested for about an hour in that cosy little pub before contemplating our next moves. Inwardly, I reflected that – despite the weather and challenges that might lie ahead – experiencing the outdoors again had already provided a boost to my spirits. You'll soon realise that, despite my moans about the weather – plus having to cope with a bad sense of direction and a fear of heights – deep down I love every minute of being outside. Sometimes just knowing I'm going for a walk is invigorating in itself. If you love doing something that is also good for your soul, nothing should hold you back.

Consulting our maps once more, we decided that Mapledurham would not be our chosen target now; we'd hoof it the few extra miles west to Pangbourne, instead of doing the sensible thing and heading back to Reading.

The previous year, during our jaunts along the Berkshire-Oxfordshire border, we had grown used to routes west of Pangbourne, so this gave us a chance to link it all up from the other side. However, this time I wasn't sure we'd made the best decision; as soon as we'd stepped off the tarmacked roads,

I was back to slipping and sliding in the churning mud like the world's worst ice skater.

'We've taken a wrong turn,' Robin announced at the end of a particularly squelchy trail.

Again, we checked the maps on our phones as we constantly wiped the rain away from the screens.

'Which way?' I asked, looking for any kind of landmark dotted against the dirty grey sky.

'We need to head back and take that road off to the left. It'll get us there,' Robin told me, pointing the way.

Yes, it meant we'd have to risk tripping up as we made our way back along the gooey path while having to hold on to thorny branches, and yes, it meant keeping to tarmac instead of meandering through fields, but it also meant being on steady ground. Part of the joy of walking in the country is being completely off-road, on secluded little paths cutting through fields. Sometimes, though, tarmac provides us with the only way forward.

We stayed tight to the edge of the road as we weaved around large puddles while trying to stay clear of oncoming traffic. Sometimes the people in the vehicles would wave, and sometimes they'd pull faces; whatever they did, we mirrored their expressions back to them. The road rose up and down like an extended rollercoaster track as we braced ourselves against the increasingly heavier patter of the rain. Ploughed field after ploughed field under a dreary sky: it all merged together as we trudged slowly on.

Occasionally we would put the world to rights, discussing the matters of the day as we walked. Oftentimes, we would just talk nonsense. Basically, we'd learnt a lot about how to make the time pass on these walks.

Then, the most surreal sight hit us: a field full of llamas!

These animals were not shy like sheep, who when called are most likely to run away; these llamas were curious, choosing to stare and then walk towards us, keeping their peepers trained directly at us.

Just when I thought there may be some altercation between us and our new South American friends, however, a van pulled up at the other side of the field and the llamas headed off in search of new adventures. Random occurrences such as this can be a real boost to the spirit and can make otherwise bleak days far more bearable.

Soon, signposts for our new destination lifted our spirits further – we were now on a much busier road that snaked into Pangbourne through Whitchurch. Leafy branches arched overhead to provide a natural roof from the deluge but, for once, I didn't actually need the cover; even though I hardly ever brought it with me, for some reason I'd brought my umbrella along for this walk. Even on previous hikes in the foulest of weather, I'd never taken a brolly, but today it served as a useful shield as we rocketed past long, deep puddles in an attempt not to get soaked by the passing traffic.

As we stepped into Whitchurch, the rain began to abate. Our surroundings became more residential, and although the hills looked inviting, they would have to wait for another time.

For now, we were clearing the bridge that led to Pangbourne, to another pub and a much-needed steak sarnie.

Looking back, I really was rather loose with my diet from the start.

Still, 11 miles done and we'd even reached the trailblazing heights of 178 metres.

A few days later, Aaron announced on the phone that he'd sustained an injury.

'My ankle went as I stepped off the kerb.'

'How bad is it?' I asked.

'Swollen and painful. It's the same ankle as before,' he replied.

Aaron had gone over on the same body part back in October 2017, when it had caused him problems for weeks.

'It'll delay me, but I should be alright,' he mentioned hopefully.

'As long as you're okay for Ben Nevis.'

'Yeah, it'll be grand. How are you getting on?'

I explained how I'd been keeping fit and that Robin and I had been on our first hike of the year, as well as describing our discussion on the potential dilemmas with winter walks.

'Before doing my ankle in, I wasn't able to jog across fields; I had to stick with street running. Not that it's done me any good,' he bemoaned.

I paused for a few seconds; what he'd said had triggered something in my mind. 'We used to run in all sorts of weather when we lived in Slough,' I reminded him.

'Twenty years ago that, mate. You wouldn't go out jogging now, would you?' Aaron said.

'No, I'm too self-conscious now. But I'd walk it.'

'Eh? We all walk around towns?' he questioned.

'No, I mean there might be a way to do a long walk in winter regardless of the weather,' I answered, with what I believed to be a sprinkle of clarity in my voice.

'You've lost me,' sighed Aaron.

'I think I've found a way to make street walks fun. Thanks, Aaron – I need to think it through a bit, but this chat has really helped.'

There was a pause before he said, 'Errrr, okay. Speak to you soon.'

Handy Tips

Whilst it's true that my paper map reading abilities are woefully limited – and while a lot of experienced hiking websites and books will tell you that such skills are essential in order to negotiate the countryside and mountainous areas – I've found that plotting walks using Google Maps can be fun. I also like to use the Street View options for certain sections of walks, as it gives me an idea of any surrounding landmarks I can look to in case we get lost. The only drawback is that it may take away the surprise of seeing a monument or stately home, say, for the first time. However, for reasons that will become clear later on, being prepared and cautious is essential – especially for an airhead like me. I'd even go as far as to say there's a certain joy in creating DIY routes, as it gives the whole walk a real personal element to it.

Chapter Five

THE LONDON ONE

Thinking back on it, I'd left Aaron in a slight state of bewilderment. You see, once the cogs start whirring inside my brain, igniting the imaginings of a new idea, I always become very keen to start working on it right away, speaking almost incoherently as I flit from one thought to the next. Sparks fly in all directions as I try to grab little nuggets of inspiration to propel the idea forward, and I find it extremely hard to settle until I've arrived at a clear – if basic – plan.

Each year, I take my birthday off work and try to do something fun on my own. It's a mini escape before returning back to reality the next day. I did a big day out in London for my fortieth a few years ago, having spent ages planning where I wanted to go. I'd been on my feet a lot that day, taking in the British Museum, Chinatown, and Borough Market, and it was this day out that provided the foundation for what I was about to propose to Robin.

I contacted him a day or two later and we loosely discussed a few initial ideas about what to do and where to go, agreeing that a change in mindset around a city walk would be a good thing, as we could then keep up with our hiking endeavours in most kinds of weather. Being constantly surrounded by people while strolling in urban areas was part of the reason we escaped for rural adventures, but one-off forays into the world of tarmac and concrete could actually do us a good turn. As for being amongst hordes of people, we'd just have to suck it up and get on with it.

Would we find a blissful zen in one of the busiest cities in the world?

A couple of Saturdays after our previous walk to Pangbourne, I met Robin on a chilly, overcast morning at the top of my street. His eyes were puffy and his hoarse voice announced he'd been hit with a cold. Despite me saying we could have held off on the walk, though, he was keen to battle on.

The train chugged through stations such as Slough, Hayes & Harlington, and Southall, the charcoal grey sky a foreboding sign that we'd made a decent choice in avoiding the countryside. As we got closer to Paddington the train became packed, filling with people wrapped in winter coats, hats, and gloves. It was so full the volume of the conversations around us made it difficult for us to hear each other.

'So,' Robin said, leaning across the table so I could hear, 'remind me: how is this, specifically, going to be good mountain training?'

I explained the idea I had about visiting museums and other places of interest via tube stations – and all the stairs that would involve.

'Plus, a good stroll around a park would mean we see at least a bit of countryside,' Robin added, tapping a band on his wrist.

'What's that?' I asked.

'My stepometer,' he replied. 'We can see how far we go; thirty-thousand steps should do it.'

'Hey, we'll be knackered!' I exclaimed. 'How far is that? Will you last out?'

'I think it's about fifteen miles or so, give or take,' Robin replied, shrugging. 'A brisk stroll will sort things out, no worries.'

As we stepped off the train, it seemed we'd be following the familiar pattern of a lot of our walks: doing something moderately different from what we'd planned to do.

As London began to swallow us up – towers and office blocks becoming the dominant features of our urban landscape – we chatted more about the advantages of London as a walking destination: having the option of visiting museums would mean we'd stay dry in seriously dodgy weather (as well as giving us the opportunity to learn stuff); the pavements offered a better walkway for our endeavours than muddy fields, particularly at this time of year; and we definitely wouldn't be short of a pub or two.

Alighting at Paddington, we battled through endless droves of people, heading to the stuffy underground before catching the tube to Marble Arch.

'Race you!' declared Robin as he bolted up the long set of stairs between the escalators.

'Wait up!' I called out. 'I thought you were unwell!'

The flat-out race provided an unexpected challenge that saw me get completely whipped, and we both felt the effects of it right away, leaning over with our hands on our knees as we gasped for breath. Passing onlookers seemed either baffled or amused by our spontaneous actions and, personally, it reminded me that Ben Nevis would not be a sprint.

Going up so many stairs had also left me feeling dizzy: about two-thirds of the way up they'd merged into one and I'd needed to slow down. This state of disorientation would repeat itself throughout the day as we descended to and ascended from the Underground. It was extremely tiring, but I took heed of the fact that anything like this would be good for me in terms of addressing any future heights that needed to be scaled.

Stepping out of the station at around 1 p.m., we eyed Hyde Park, imbued in sunshine. Although initially confused by the happy turn in the weather, we weren't going to grumble; as hats and gloves were hastily removed, we realised we could now be far more outdoorsy than originally planned. The museums could wait for another day.

Hyde Park could have been a day out in itself, especially as families, joggers, and dog walkers were all out in droves, enjoying the sunshine and fresh air. We patrolled anti-clockwise, starting from near Speakers' Corner and heading around the stretch of track known as The Ring, which bordered the tree-lined open parkland. There were many pathways dissecting through the grass and I thought we could probably have notched up a few miles if we traced them all out.

Early on, we espied horses and riders honing their equestrian skills, and although we contemplated going further westward to Kensington Gardens, we instead turned left and marched down to The Serpentine lake. Here, on its north side, we stopped to watch folk boating on the water, which reflected the bright winter sun. People slurped at ice creams, adding another layer of escape to this rather surreal mini heatwave. As we skirted past various statues, a bandstand, and a rose garden, I thought that if we hadn't charged ourselves with an urban expedition, Hyde Park would have provided many quiet spaces for contemplation. Finally, we completed our lap along a long stretch of path adjacent to Park Lane, before heading back to the start.

'We could've actually been out in the country in this weather,' I said, daydreaming of all the many hills waiting to be walked. 'Still, this place is great.'

'It was good. Plus, we've done over four miles already,' Robin offered wearily, his adrenaline levels sapping as we headed back to the tube station. 'I need to eat soon.'

'Borough Market?' I suggested.

'Go on then. I'll hold out,' Robin replied.

I studied the tube map, promptly forgot the route, and then checked again, confused. Just before I went to ask one of the staff for directions, Robin indicated that he knew where we were going: Marble Arch to London Bridge with a change at Bond Street. Had I been making this trip by myself, I would have had to ask somebody at Bond Street as well as checking my phone for directions.

We managed to survive several overpacked, sweat-inducing carriages, many more steps, and my dodgy sense of direction, and eventually we found the market.

I'd been here a couple of times before and I revelled at being back among the hustle and bustle, where the aromas of fresh produce met with a bouquet of world cuisine through a maze of stalls that caused our senses to buzz. We tried free samples of meat, bread, and cheese, and pressing on through the swarms, we arrived at another stall and each bought paella. Robin also bought a pie ('feed a cold, starve a fever,' he said) before we shuffled on out of the market. We sat on a side street kerb next to some other market-goers, and wolfed down the heart-warming meal as the sun shone down on us.

Now, you could argue that walking around a market doesn't really count as being part of a hike, but we would differ in opinion. The fact is that you can easily get lost in the many exciting sights of London, ambling about and not really being aware of how many steps you're racking up. So, although this culinary diversion didn't exactly help with the calorie count, it certainly helped with the step count.

After a brief stop at nearby Southwark Cathedral, Robin announced that the meal had invigorated him and that, for the last leg, we should march along the South Bank. Late afternoon soon became early evening, bringing along a sharp drop in temperature, and hats and gloves were adorned once more.

Along main streets, side streets, up steps, down steps, and around and about, we attempted to reach our 30,000 steps. We held tight along the Thames by the South Bank for a duration, exhaling plumes of cold breath as people glided by in all directions: some aimless, some with purpose, others with oodles of time. We paused briefly to grab a tea from a riverside kiosk, the hot liquid bringing some much-needed warmth to our bodies.

We became so driven in our attempt to reach 30,000 steps that I lost track of the route we'd taken and the landmarks we'd passed; London had also begun to take on a labyrinthine quality under the cola-black night as the tall, dark buildings started to look awesome and foreboding.

We were just nearing Waterloo Station when we hit our target number of steps and, now overwhelmed with tiredness, I couldn't work out why my money wasn't being accepted by the entry-exit barrier to the public toilet. I cussed as I felt my bladder about to give out, and it was only when a helpful bloke told me I was putting my money in the change machine rather than the slot to move through the turnstile that I realised my error.

The funny thing about the London walk was that, although it involved a lot more sitting down – on the tube, for instance – I ached more afterwards than I had from the Pangbourne walk. Perhaps it was all the stairs, I'm not sure.

It was mentally uplifting carving out our own adventure in the city, and the numbers of people weren't really a bother as we maintained focus on what we were doing. We'd found a level of escape and spontaneity in a most unexpected way. We also had enormous fun. I think I'd feel differently if I was stuck in a large city all the time, and personally I find the countryside to be a more preferred location for our walking endeavours, but still… London had shifted our mindsets slightly. It had given us an all-weather destination that, from time to time, would provide us with a valuable and much-needed backup option.

Handy Tips

Buy a guidebook on Britain, pick a town or city, then head out and explore.

Design your own day out by doing an internet search for locations of interest, then plan the transport links to each one – or just walk to them. Use Tripadvisor to search locations and places of interest.

Be spontaneous: turn up in a random location and see where the day takes you.

Chapter Six

THE BEAST FROM THE EAST KNOCKS US OFF OUR FEET

The end of February and start of March brought major bouts of snow in the form of the dreaded Beast from the East, thus proving true Robin's concerns of a dodgy winter impacting our regular hikes.

With a combination of despair and awe, I watched day by day from my kitchen window as the world was painted pure white again and again. The indoors became the new outdoors as I settled for doing workouts in my living room. I'd wanted to go for a bigger trek in the snow – even just for a few miles around the local streets – but the fact that I'd twice already gone base-over-apex on the way to the local shops had put me off venturing outside: during those brief trips out, only the rucksack on my back had prevented me from sustaining any kind of injury.

So, I came up with another fitness plan, of sorts: after seeing Robin's stepometer do us proud in London, I'd bought a cheap one and tried to reach 10,000 steps (a little under five miles) a day – as that seemed to be the suggested quota these days – by simply walking around my house. I bounded in and out of rooms, zigzagged around the kitchen, and pounded up and down the stairs – for a few days, anyway. Then I went back to looking out the kitchen window, watching icicles form on branches, and observing small birds salvaging for scraps under the softly blanketed garden.

My keep-fit routines kept me going, yet every day I yearned to step out into the wilderness. Robin and I did actually manage to meet one Saturday in early March for a few hours' walk around Reading town centre, killing time in and out of stores in a retail park; a hobby store, a sofa store, and an outdoor specialist store all provided shelter from the bitingly cold conditions outside, as well as bumping up our steps until we rewarded ourselves with a hot, hearty, all-day breakfast.

By mid-March, the snow had melted and my walking aspirations had returned. When I was a kid, the snow had always seemed like such a big, wonderful adventure; now, it's an inconvenience to travel or walking plans. Call me a grump or whatever – that's just how I feel.

After the enforced hiatus, my solo weekday walks took on an added vigour, and I did no less than four miles of an evening. As I became fitter, I also had better recovery, and I felt like doing at least some exercise most days.

Meanwhile, Aaron had begun to jog again after doing his ankle in.

'Don't push it, mate,' Robin joked during a video chat one evening when I was round his house.

'True. I guess we're only walking up,' Aaron replied.

Walking and being out and about had further strengthened our bond; here we were now supporting each other to become physically fitter, more determined than ever to take our hiking pursuits even further. Having a new shared passion after so many years of friendship is great; with walking, our bond is reinvigorated each time we go somewhere new, with the fresh experiences cultivating a wealth of memories every time.

I was raring to go – that was, until I got zapped by a mystery illness around the late middle part of the month.

The symptoms of this condition were strange and complex. Imagine you're just about getting over a heavy cold; you're weak, listless, achy, and your brain has become nothing more than pummelled marshmallow. Well, this mystery illness featured those exact symptoms – just without the cold. What makes it more of a mystery is that, with this illness, you can carry on doing your normal day-to-day affairs, but only in a very half-a-job way; to an outsider, you could look incompetent, uncaring even.

I'd first been struck by this bunch of ailments as a 15-year-old, when the only way I'd been able to describe it to my GP during a home visit – yep, my doc did a home visit just for me feeling a bit washed out! – was that 'I just think I'm a bit ill or something'.

There was also a two-week period in February 1995 when I swear these symptoms hit me again, this time when I was half-way through my second year at university in Wales: I'd sleep through morning lectures, wake up in time for *Neighbours*, then go back to bed. The only difference was that this time around I would wake up again in the evening feeling totally revived and head off down to the pub, only to find the symptoms returning as I stirred in my bed the following day. Or maybe this was because I was a lazy, hungover student – I'm not sure.

This time around the mystery ailment was well and truly brewing, and as I knew I couldn't push myself as much, I decided to stick only to my necessary work and household tasks until I rode out this bout of questionable health. The upshot of this was that I was suddenly transported from being a moderately healthy person with big aspirations into having an apathetic, tiresome kind of half-life.

As the days wore on, I became more and more concerned that I wouldn't be able to make the proposed walk with Robin on the last Saturday of the month. Having not ventured into the countryside for a few weeks by this point, I found myself becoming tetchier as the days wore on. After the shambles that the Beast from the East had caused, we were desperate to get ourselves back out into rural Berkshire, as much fun as London had been.

Robin and I messaged back and forth, trying to decide on a course of action.

The mystery illness finally worked its way out of my system around midweek, leaving me with a residual tiredness. The usual walk to and from work was my only exercise; even then, my body ached as if I'd been put through a mangle. All my previous training seemed worthless now; my fitness had decreased and, for the time being, I could only motivate myself so much.

At least I could now focus more on writing, but writing about walking made me think about walking, and that made me want to walk for miles.

By Friday, though, my bones were a bit more refreshed and raring for adventure; I'd been busy with work all week and now I needed to rejuvenate myself. So, ignoring my body's desire for a slow recovery, and with no planned hike with Robin the following day – we'd postponed due to the mystery illness – I packed a snack and drink in my backpack with two mini missions in mind: to push myself and to find the nearest patch of green land.

After thinking for a bit, I planned a sojourn to a local thicket just west of Maidenhead. The trip would take me along an A-road, and I'd have just enough daylight to scout out the venue for future walks; I had an hour each way before nightfall, which I thought would be enough time for a little recon.

Leaving the house, I strode past a row of shops and several leafless trees, showing the death mark of winter. I then turned on to the A-road, where the volume and noise of the traffic hit me in an instant, making me worry that the distraction would reduce the pleasantness of the walk. Some of our long walks incorporated a section of motorway, but we would always try to keep this to a minimum – for obvious reasons. Now, I was mentally kicking myself for missing the obvious drawback to this route: it was all along the A-road. Not just in part. And in rush hour. I'd been aware of it; I just hadn't completely thought it through.

Then, as I began to contemplate a new approach, I noticed a public footpath I'd not been down before. Although the gnarls of winter were still clinging on, it was a passably mild spring afternoon that saw beams of sunlight flitting through a fluffy cloud layer, and my mood became light and curious as I delighted in the spontaneity and diversion this footpath offered.

I started walking down it, and soon I'd left behind the drone of passing vehicles; now, the only sound I could hear was the patter of my own feet across the soft, dry mud.

The footpath snaked its way through the backs of houses running parallel to each other, the waft of creosote off back garden fences almost making my nostrils and eyes burn as it pervaded the length of the alley.

As I ambled along I noticed several side paths coming off the main one I was on, giving the area a labyrinthine quality reminiscent of the 1980-90s children's TV show *Knightmare*. So, as I continued on my way I recalled the imagination of my youth, fighting off goblins and trading information with wizards in exchange for a spell.

After just 15 minutes I came out by a small glen next to the A-road, and although my diversion had only been brief, it surprised me how free and loose I was able to feel in such a short space of time.

I now had a choice: I could carry on along my intended path towards the thicket, or turn left to where I could see open fields. I chose the latter due to a fast-developing curiosity to see unexplored territory. The thicket could wait!

On the outskirts of Maidenhead, the farm fields looked incredibly inviting. However, as sundown was less than an hour away, I had to remind myself: this was a scouting mission only.

A line of trees formed a border to the scenery beyond, broken up by the odd farmhouse here and there. Again, I felt the rush I only ever sensed in the open air; today, though, I'd have to settle for being a passive observer from the edge of civilisation.

I headed further up the road until I reached the corner opposite a cosy-looking country pub, which I knew would make a welcome pit stop on a future walk.

Now it was time for the return leg. By the time I reached home I'd only been walking for 70 minutes, yet I felt mentally refreshed while my body felt energised: perhaps I'd walked out the remnants of the mystery illness.

There were many bonuses to this walk that I would never have anticipated as I stepped out for just a short while. The town took on a different meaning as I noticed I was interacting with it in a different, mindful way. I also felt detached and relaxed as I knew I was doing something different from all the others rushing about in their busy lives.

Solo walks can be fun. Normally, I'd go for an evening walk simply to keep up momentum, but this one began to make me think of my hometown in a different way.

The extra significance of this walk was that it served as a way to banish the ups-and-downs of the last few weeks of snow – and of feeling crud – and it also made me embrace all the possibilities spring could offer.

Now we could begin to focus on finding more hills to climb in preparation for Ben Nevis.

I hope this chapter shows that by simply sticking on your trainers and heading out for a bit around your local area, gaining a fresh perspective is possible – and incredibly rewarding. Try to notice the trees, the flowers, and the wildlife more than you usually would, and look at them from a different angle, with fresh eyes. This could even be achieved on a simple walk to or from work – it just requires a change of mindset. Since that outing I've done many solo walks around my town with this attitude shift, and it's so good for restoring mental well-being when an instant hit of calm is needed.

Chapter Seven

SHAME: RAIN AGAIN!

The 70-minute walk had lifted my spirits enormously, as well as adding an extra revitalising layer to my evening walks. With each passing day I became physically better, and although my body cried out for a slow recovery, I became determined: nothing would prevent me from trekking the 14 miles Robin and I had planned for the last Friday in March.

Thanks to the weather, this would be our first proper expedition in a couple of months. Urban settings had secured their place as alternative hikes during the snowy season – and we'd learnt so much by doing this – but now it was time to pack the rucksack and get out amongst the hills, valleys, rivers and forests once more. Ben Nevis was beginning to feel more tangible again, and – as long as the conditions continued to be decent – we'd savour each and every outing in its own right. Still, at least a walk or two in the snow, plus the biting cold, would count as some kind of preparation if we ended up facing wicked weather on the day we took on the mountain.

On the morning of our end of March walk, I woke up with a real sense of anticipation. I dressed quickly, wolfed down a coffee, and confirmed the last-minute arrangements with Robin before bounding down the road to the train station.

As the train picked up speed past the edges of town, I basked in the thought that the problems the topsy-turvy weather had brought us were no more – even though ominous dark clouds were currently hanging in the sky – and as I watched the houses whizz by, the sense of adventure and possibility gripped me once again. Walking really does gift the mind, body, and soul with a fuel for life.

At Reading station, I spotted Robin and waved to him as he weaved and bobbed around the peeps on the escalator.

'Are you ready for this?' he said with a grin as he walked over.

'More than ready,' I replied, my anticipation now reaching a crescendo.

The shared buzz of being out and about in order to entertain our rural pursuits was palpable from the off as we boarded another train, leaving behind the throngs for the tranquillity of the Oxfordshire countryside.

After a short journey, we arrived at Cholsey station and took to light-footing through the neat village streets until we found a signpost that would take us to the Thames Path. Soon, the murky waters of the river came into view as we headed into the countryside.

This marked the proper start of our route, which we'd done previously in preparation for Snowdon back in 2017; it was one of those self-created ones that comes about by letting your feet take you wherever they want to go.

Although I attempted to blank out the foreboding skies above, my heart sank as we turned onto the boggy path; thick mud – with the consistency of chocolate gateaux and cream – clung to my boots as, yet again, I tottered 20 paces behind Robin, clutching fences and branches to save me from falling. To our left, our old friend the river followed its course; to our right, the farm fields glistened after a night-time downpour. Trying to take in the scenery, however, only served as a brief distraction as I found myself constantly scrambling for safety.

Had I learnt nothing from that walk to Pangbourne back in the winter? If I couldn't cope with a flat, muddy path, then how on earth would I fare making my way up Britain's greatest mountain?

Best to just hold on and ride this one out, I told myself.

I hadn't had the practice due to the bad weather, but now was the time to focus. Unfortunately, I'd forgotten how dodgy I could be on my pins.

This instant reawakening to my limitations, however, somehow spurred me on.

It sounds crazy because this was only a mucky footpath, but often my brain turns mushier than the surfaces I'm navigating my way across. On Scafell Pike, I'd cursed myself for not being as sure-footed as I'd like to be, but my friends had waited and willed me on and we had eventually achieved our shared goal together. Those instances encouraged me to become more solid on my feet, so I had to change my mindset and way of seeing things: this muddy path wasn't an obstacle, but instead a challenge to be overcome. (There's another mental health benefit to being outdoors: pushing yourself and developing perseverance to break through both physical and mental barriers.)

Thankfully, the path became more bearable after about a mile and a half, which was a good thing as the rain was now well and truly forcing itself down on us. My initial elation at being out in the countryside had begun to ebb, so I bolstered myself with the thought that my new waterproofs would withstand the test, making this day out at least a bit better than bearable (after all, sometimes it's the small comforts that keep you going). However, the dodgy weather stayed with us all day as we were pummelled with solid sheets of unending rain. We'd known there was a chance of inclement weather when we started out, but we hadn't realised it would be quite this bad.

'We need to find cover,' commented Robin as we made our way along the road to the village of Moulsford.

'Time to pick up the pace,' I replied.

After having covered subjects such as football, village life, and our Ben Nevis preparation, the conversation became reduced to sound bites relating to the conditions as we steeled ourselves in an attempt to find somewhere warm and dry.

'Fourteen miles of this…really?' I moaned.

'It's like the Mapledurham-turned-Pangbourne walk all over again,' said Robin. 'Let's find somewhere to stop and re-evaluate.'

'Okay,' I agreed, 'a shop would be good; I've forgotten to bring a drink.'

So, as I took to catching fast-falling raindrops on my tongue in a poor attempt to battle my thirst, we blitzed past a pub (closed!), a church, and a cricket pitch. Soon we'd passed through Moulsford and had found ourselves on the other side of the Thames.

At the start of the walk from Cholsey it had been great to see hardly a soul about, but now it became a source of comfort to see others: dog walkers greeted us as we made our way up the muddy riverside track, while families and couples waved from boats plodding lazily up the river. These guys certainly weren't letting the weather hold them back, and things like this can be a huge motivator when you find yourself out on a hike in cruddy weather: for just a brief second you can find yourself united with strangers, feeling like you're accomplishing something together.

Riverside homes began to dominate the view now, reminding us that – despite the brief sense of camaraderie we'd found – we still needed to find a safe haven. Trees provided zero shelter as droplets perpetually splashed us from bare overhanging branches, so we soon moved off the main towpath and into marshy fields, where grumpy cows stared at us as we passed. Only when the bridge that joined Goring and Streatley appeared did we hasten our pace.

At around 12.30 p.m. we found a table at a snug café on Goring High Street, taking a break to check our hiking vital signs: despite our coats being soaked, we were dry and now warming up. Most importantly, our mobiles hadn't become drenched; something I learnt from our other rain-soaked adventure back in early February was to bring a small waterproof bag (a sandwich bag is fine) with me to protect my mobile in shoddy weather.

In that moment I felt thankful that it was just the two of us doing this route, as the last thing we'd need in a situation like this was some bossy hiking group organiser saying we needed to see this walk through to the bitter end. That kind of attitude is okay – and we've been doggedly determined on many of our treks before and since – but sometimes, when you want to call it a day, the last thing you need is an overbearing busybody trying to have total control.

When our fry-ups came we munched them down quick time. Somebody on another table had left behind a half-finished crossword, so we attempted to complete it whilst waiting for the downpour to pass.

But it didn't pass.

And so we waited.

And waited.

And drank more tea.

And waited.

'Do you think we've escaped the zombie hordes?' I asked.

'They don't care about the weather; they're right on our tail,' Robin answered with a sense of resignation.

'Crumbs! We need to start hot-stepping it again soon,' I replied, peering nervously through the window for our nemeses.

'Aye, we need a plan,' considered Robin.

Since our early walks, we'd conceived the idea that we had to endure all this walking as a means of eternally escaping zombies, aliens, dinosaurs, or any other potential make-believe threat to humanity. These are just a few of the techniques that provide us with a source of comical motivation when conditions are against us. Other techniques include us being back in our own homes in time to watch the Emmerdale omnibus on TV.

'So, what are the options here?' Robin asked.

'We keep walking...or we hop on the train,' I offered.

'Shall we check what times the trains run from Goring to Reading?'

'Yeah.'

'Zombies don't know how to buy train tickets,' Robin pointed out, 'so we should be safe there.'

His sage wisdom proved correct, and soon we'd boarded a train back to Reading. We could have carried on like we did in Pangbourne – and I'm sure there'll be times in the future when we do – but this day wasn't that day. Perhaps the weather won. Or perhaps it was because we'd warmed up nicely in the café and wanted to maintain that feeling. Most likely, though, we didn't want to be overrun by a gang of the undead.

Still, we'd done six and a half miles, even if this first joint foray after our hiatus had begun with enthusiasm but ended with resignation.

After I said goodbye to Robin at Reading, a concern rose up in me that the walks section of this book would only entail country treks in the rain or alternative city walks because of bad weather – which, I suppose, is par for the course when you live in England.

Sure, we'd found that experiencing adverse weather and considering walking alternatives can be uplifting for the soul, but to crave sunshine after the past few weeks was no bad thing.

Chapter Eight

BEACON HILL BONANZA

March eventually ended and April brought with it the hope of brighter weather. Despite this upturn in circumstances, however, one of the age-old issues of the male of the species took over again: partially planning things, but never seeing them through. Dates were agreed between Robin and I for hikes, only for replies to be slow both ways, due to planning around family life or because of urgent matters that needed attention – such as finding a new series to watch on Netflix or daydreaming about what would be a secure enough location on Slough Trading Estate to hide a tin of sweetcorn.

I carried on with plenty of street walks as the weather became generally better, the mystery illness now – thankfully – well and truly behind me. My 'snackercise' regime was also well under way; it had become a philosophy of sorts after Robert had imparted the necessary wisdom to me. 'Push myself that bit harder,' I'd tell myself, 'there's a scotch egg waiting at the end of this.'

I began to watch more and more videos on YouTube about walking up Ben Nevis – it interested me to see the perspectives of several different people on how they tackled the big hike – and I also read up on the route on a few websites (I've included a couple in the Appendix for convenience). I did such activities mainly because I needed to mentally prepare myself for the heights, but sometimes this did me more harm than good. There were times when I'd watch somebody calmly swaggering up Ben Nevis and my hands would become clammy from seeing all of Creation spread out far below.

'It's good to be prepared,' Aaron remarked over the phone one mid-April evening. 'I committed like that for Scafell Pike. Nowadays, though, I only do the necessaries to prepare.'

'Like what?' I enquired.

'I usually read up on the route, check out some maps, and see what kind of weather makes it dangerous.'

'Yeah, we've enough experience between us to be aware of the precautions we should take,' I added.

'I purposefully stay away from videos or pics of the walk now as I want to experience it all for the first time when we arrive,' admitted Aaron. 'You do what you do, though, 'cause that's what's right for you.'

'Cheers, mate. Here, have you heard about the Ben Nevis Webcam?' I asked.

'No.'

'It's a website with regular weather updates. Today Ben is covered in cloud,' I informed him.

'Cool, send us a link. That'll be handy to keep an eye on now and again.'

I'd found the Ben Nevis Webcam whilst checking out weather reports a few days before, and from then right up until we left, I regularly shared the weather updates on our social media chat group.

Eventually, after a few weeks' hiatus, Robin and I managed to sort a Saturday at the end of April for a day excursion he'd researched. When we met up, I mentioned to him how I'd been preparing.

'I can understand that,' Robin concurred as we strolled from the car park near the top of Beacon Hill to start our walk. 'For me, as long as there's a decent path up and the weather's okay, I'm sorted. I just want to enjoy the thrill when I'm there.'

'Yeah, I think Robert and Aaron are the same.'

Robert in particular always has this quiet reassurance about him; his long-distance running has made him confident to simply turn up and take on the mountains. So, whilst I'm sweating it out pondering the contours, gradients, and slopes of all our treks, experience has taught me it's a bonus to have three calm friends to share the adventures with.

Before we started, Robin and I scanned the area from the top of Beacon Hill to make sure all around was zombie-free. This was the start of an eight and a half mile circular in the Surrey Hills, and although the day had brought thick clouds and a threat of rain, this time we'd brought a change of clothes and Robin had chosen a semi-self-created route that meandered off the main National Trust route – one that included several pub stops.

We began with an amble past the cairn that marked the top of the hill, and then through woodland that gave out to views of a bowl-shaped valley with open grassland, steep ups, steep downs, sheep, cows, and hardly anybody in sight. The hills were alive with the sound of walking!

Soon, the necessary sounds of birdsong and the wind rustling through the trees replaced the town sounds of honking horns and revving vehicles. Despite the lack of sun all the greens, browns, yellows, purples, and blues of the flora and fauna seemed so vivid; this, along with the passing aroma of the plants and flowers, soon put me into a state of calm that only these treks can provide.

This ramble was a good test on the legs, as we encountered several inclines that demanded the best of us. We passed other walkers and wished them well, although we considered the plight of one poor individual when we noticed a pair of abandoned trousers on a fence post. It reminded us of a song called 'Where are my trousers?' that I'd written with another friend called James in the early 1990s. Played along to a demo tune on my brother's keyboard, it was a dodgy rap with a chorus belted out in a gruff voice that made me sound like I'd just chain-smoked fifty fags and had no intention of stopping.

The landscape became flatter now, and as we crested one final hill that curiously formed part of somebody's back garden, we made it to our first village and, most importantly, our first pub.

As we sat outside, supping our beers and watching small insects skitter on the water, it was reassuring to know we could replicate this feat further along our trail – something that made up for us not being allowed into the actual bar, as there was a private function on. With the additional bonus of zero rainfall so far, we really did appreciate these small mercies, especially given all the previous haphazard weather we'd faced so far that year.

After we'd finished our pints we set off again, heading out onto the tree-lined route of the Meon Valley Trail. To our right, views expanded across ripe fields; to our left, there was nothing more than boggy woodland. A couple we could see far in the distance provided us with the motivation to zip through this part of the journey: it was now necessary to take them over as a true mark of our physical development. This plan promptly failed, however, as I had to stop a couple of times to tie my laces, which resulted in our new adversaries disappearing out of view.

Instead, we chatted about an even greater rival: Ben Nevis. We agreed that we were better prepared than ever to take on the mountain; our new fitness regimes had become so ingrained in our day-to-day lives that the idea of training for the adventure had actually become addictively enjoyable.

I did, however, have one concern – my ongoing fear of heights – and I relayed this worry to Robin. At least, given all the research I'd done and all the friends I'd talked to who'd been up the Ben, I knew I was better prepared than last time. Heights or not, I'd get there – I'd just have to take it slow, if I needed to, in order to finish the job. Rather philosophically, Robin added that the real enemy was not the mountain for the mountain does not care; no, we are only limited to what we think we can or can't do.

All this talk marked a stark contrast to the faith I'd had in myself at the start of the year: fitness and heights were my greatest fears and I'd dreaded tackling Britain's highest peak, but now I was looking forward to it. I just had to do my best, and if it became too much I'd take a break or even stop – and there's no shame in that. After all this walking we'd done over the past couple of years, experience had taught me that even if a journey isn't completed, at least it's been attempted, and that's enough.

Soon, we left the footpath and, after a short country road, we entered the village of West Meon. Here we found another country pub with nice squishy armchairs and a fireplace that could only have been more welcoming if a roaring blaze had greeted us on entry.

As we relaxed back in our seats we noticed a set of stuffed squirrels with petrified faces in a glass case running the length of the bar – and they were playing cricket! The other clientele – a mix of families, couples, and other walkers – seemed oblivious to the terrified creatures posing above us. All of this perplexed us more than why my shoelaces kept coming undone, then it distracted us for a bit, then we simply gave up and consoled ourselves with beer.

After leaving the pub we resumed our journey, taking a turn through a churchyard before going down a side road to begin the final leg of our route. Something, however, wasn't quite right. There was an anomaly between the scenery described in the online walking guide and what we were actually looking at.

The guide stated that we should be clinging to the edge of a meadow, soon to ascend a hill, yet we were actually standing at the edge of a cul-de-sac that formed part of a housing estate.

This can actually happen quite a lot. Sometimes, it's because the routes we find from websites haven't been updated for some time, which can lead to much confusion. This is why having a fully charged phone and portable charger with you at the start of a walk is essential, as at least you can then refer to the maps on your phone. Taking paper maps with you can be handy if there's no phone reception, but we have – rather inexplicably – never found ourselves in that situation. I guess it's because we feel that, as long as we have access to the maps on our phones, we'll be okay. I'm sure any seasoned hiker would roll their eyes reading that; what would happen if we became lost – truly lost – and had no reception or battery? Take heed, dear reader: boost your map-reading and compass skills.

As we stood there consulting the maps on our phones, I remarked to Robin that we must have looked like a couple of ne'er-do-wells seeking out some kind of dodgy deal. Thankfully, a kind bloke in his fifties passed us and gave us the right directions, and we were able to match what he said with the route described. This meant that, in this case, the online guide was up to date; we'd simply ventured off course.

As you've probably guessed by now, I find it hard to follow directions; I can remember the names of landmarks we need to pass in order to reach the destination, yet my brain gives out when I'm told how to find a place. Fortunately, Robin has the reverse affliction, so we were soon strolling through fields due to a co-dependence to find our way back to the car. And I swear we saw the man who'd given us directions pass us once or twice in his car – or in a few different cars. Was he the guardian angel of hikers making sure we'd taken the right path?

The last section gave us some much-needed hills as we skirted through more picturesque villages, went past a trout farm, then found ourselves in fields full of watercress, before making the final ascent through sloping farmland to the top of a prominence that gave exhilarating views of a fertile basin below. Just to be there and take in the vista brought me a much-needed head-clearing moment.

Gravity went against us now as we trudged up Beacon Hill from the other side, as if there were puppet strings reaching out of the ground a few yards ahead, pulling us along. At around 260 metres high the hill provided us with a good test, as well as providing me with a confidence boost before the weekend in Scotland; however, we would need to do this height more than five times over to reach the summit of Ben Nevis.

Eventually we found our way back to the car, having completed a rural escapade which had, for once, been unaffected by horrendous weather.

How many more hills could be scaled before we took on the Mighty One in June?

Chapter Nine

WILL THE REAL WALBURY HILL PLEASE STAND UP?

Not long after the Beacon Hill walk, it occurred to me that I'd not really fulfilled an earlier promise I'd made to myself of going as high as I could. Hills of 250-300 metres were good to build the legs, and given that my friends and I could only meet every couple of weeks to do day trips, it was the best we could do.

Sure, I'd watched videos of going up high mountains, but that could only prepare me so much. I'd thought about going to a climbing centre, doing a hot air balloon ride, or basically trying anything else that would test me and my fear of heights, but these ideas didn't really appeal to me (or I couldn't afford them).

Fortunately, Robert was on hand yet again to provide his on-the-spot wisdom during a curry night in Reading in early May.

'Fitness isn't an issue for you,' he said.

'No, it's the heights thing that can drain me,' I admitted.

'Time is an issue too, going far enough to do bigger hills.'

'Yeah, that and money,' I replied, puzzled.

'Well, just do what you're doing with local hills and don't fret about it. You'll complete Ben Nevis no problem. You might be a bit slower than you'd like, but that's okay. Just accept it and enjoy the journey,' he smiled. Robert has always been good at seeing the best in a situation and accepting it for what it is.

Having pondered that advice, I arranged with Robin to return to where it all began: on the late May Bank Holiday of 2016, we'd embarked on our first hike proper to Walbury Hill.

Situated near the village of Inkpen in West Berkshire, this hill is the highest natural point in South East England. We'd been extremely unprepared for that debut journey, illustrated by the fact that we'd done the walk in trainers and jeans. This hadn't been fun, as a persistent rain had battered us from start to finish – now there's a surprise! – causing me to slip and slide about, and at one point I'd even lost the contents of my wallet.

Still, being able to say we'd reached the top of a particular hill had provided us with at least some sense of achievement, and the fact that it was the highest in the South East provided even more. The shoddy conditions of that day had no effect on our future adventures and, ever since, we've mastered coping with different weather situations.

Robin and I reflected on all this during the train ride from Reading to Kintbury (the nearest train station to the hill). On that first offering, we'd managed seven miles with our mate Pete, stopping for a break every mile and a half or so. Now, we were attempting a brisk and linear 12-mile wander starting at

Kintbury, travelling through Inkpen, and then taking on Walbury Hill and Ham Hill before finishing at Bedwyn train station – with only one designated stop for lunch. Walking longer distances is something the body can get used to in just a short space of time.

I'd found this particular route on a walkers' website, and as we strode along the canal, past a church, and out of Kintbury, it became clear that this would be a pleasant if testing roam. We followed fence-lined pathways onto rising fields, crossed over B-roads, and skipped over streams before entering the beautiful Inkpen Nature Reserve, where we found ourselves surrounded by silver birches and a vast array of plants and wildlife.

At a clearing, the guidance notes told us to take a path to the right, near the information board – the only problem was, the information board didn't exist and, from where we stood, we could see two paths going off to the right. We thought back to the Beacon Hill walk when we'd become lost; then, we'd been able to retrace our steps thanks to our guide and the kindly gentleman's advice. Here, though, the instructions didn't match up at all to what we saw.

We read ahead, looking for any further landmarks that would give us a clue, then we pointed in various directions and shrugged our shoulders, scouring about for any knowledgeable locals. In the end, we decided that – as the instructions had only indicated to follow the right-hand path and not the 'extreme' right-hand path – we'd follow the first one. (Given this anomaly, I've not included this walk in the appendix.)

From here, the directions vaguely matched up to what we were seeing; although we weren't completely convinced of the line we were taking, we seemed to at least be following a route of sorts. However, as we exited a woodland path and emerged onto a farm field, with an air of resignation we concurred that we were, indeed, lost. Even studying the maps on our phones couldn't link us to the particular route we sought, but at least Robin noticed a nearby pub that would serve as a stopping point from which we could refocus our efforts.

Soon, over a pint and a sandwich in a leafy beer garden, I was cursing myself for taking us on an out-of-date trek. Our many excursions into the countryside had taught us that such occurrences were all part of the experience, however, and I appreciated Robin reminding me of that. Having asked a barman the way to Walbury Hill, we were boosted by receiving much clearer directions.

His suggested route took us down country lanes near to the top of the hill. This was a steady but gentle incline that afforded us the opportunity to appreciate the fields and woodland below, as well as the houses dotted about like boats on a sea of green.

Life began to slow down, so I embraced the release that I'd hoped would have come as soon as we'd alighted at Kintbury. Plus, now we weren't bound by following instructions; wherever we decided to go, it was our choice. A double dollop of freedom, then.

Up we climbed as cars passed by and, naturally, our hearts gladdened as we made the ascent. The hill came into view and the road soon gave way to a gravel-like path.

Back in 2016 we'd come by car with Pete, and as there's a car park two-thirds of the way up, at the time we felt let down that the way to the top was so easy. Now, though, we'd done a proper field trip to this county top – at least, that was, until a couple on their way down told us we were actually about to hit the top of Gallows Down and that Walbury Hill was about a quarter of a mile or so to the west.

Robin rolled his eyes and I shook my head. Not only had I sent us in the wrong direction now, but I'd also sent us wrong back in 2016 too – and that had been a supposedly well-researched project on my part in anticipation of our big expedition.

As my history of sham location finding unfurled, I quietly told myself that I should trust those with better map skills than me (again, dear reader, take notice: map and compass skills are so important). Also, up to this point we'd wrestled with the idea of resuming the initial walk to Bedwyn; however, by this time we'd already accomplished seven and a half miles – and we didn't fancy relying on instructions that might have taken us into the abyss – so we promptly ditched the idea.

Again, Robin enthused that such things just added to the spice of the adventure, plus we now had an extra hill to conquer. Despite these advantages, however, my confidence in orientation had been seriously dented.

We followed the path – which I now knew to be the Test Way – past sloping farm fields as sheep stared at us from both sides. Even though a trickle of day trippers peppered the route, we both remarked that this felt like a rather understated location. The roads that had led us here showed no signs for the hill, and there was no information board – a common theme on this walk – to show off the significance of the hill.

We found this particularly strange, as this area is drenched in history: the top of the hill was home to an Iron Age hillfort, and the Wayfarer's Walk route is said to have existed since Celtic times. As well as this, the story of Combe Gibbet, which sits atop Gallows Down, is fascinating: the gibbet was erected in 1676 to hang a man and woman who murdered the man's wife and son in order to maintain their affair, after which the gibbet was left to deter others from committing any crimes. As well as this, opposite the car park there's a plaque stating that the valley below served as a practice zone for the Normandy landings of World War Two. Walbury Hill has seen it all, standing there in quiet solitude.

To me, this whole area is a mystical, timeless place oozing with history and intrigue. It's one of my favourite places to escape, and a place that I hope to visit again and again. I'd even go so far as to say it's one of the best places I've visited.

Following the GPS on our phones, the gravel path soon turned to tarmac once more, and my head began to spin as I couldn't work out whether we were facing north, south, east, or west. Robin proffered that we'd overshot the hill; I thought we should keep going. With no pubs nearby from which to take stock and with nobody around to ask for directions again, we turned back.

Just as I was about to curse myself for not carrying a map and compass again, Robin's reasoned hunch proved correct; we checked with a horse rider, and soon we were cresting a steep incline with embankments that doubled up as a playground for sheep. As we strode atop the large, upturned, pudding bowl-shaped mound, we spotted the concrete pillar that marked the top of the hill – which was confirmed by the GPS. For once man and technology were in harmony with nature, despite me almost leading us astray again.

In a 360-degree spin I took in the whole scene, imagining that this would have been a good spot to see an enemy Iron Age tribe entering the valley. Today, though, the only defensive aids for Robin and myself against a potential attack were a feature-less brick building and a drinking trough for the sheep. Still, the scenery was staggering, with all the far-reaching valleys and fields resting under a blustery powder grey sky.

Once we were ready we wound down the other side and out through a farm gate, onto the gravel track, and along the B-roads back to Kintbury train station, hastened all the way by a steady downpour.

It had been great to finally find the real Walbury Hill amidst dodgy directions and a lack of signage, and Robin's wisdom that this all just added to the adventure actually radiated through; looking back, this journey is definitely a stand-out one for me.

In preparation for writing up this walk, I checked the internet to see if, this time, we'd actually conquered Walbury Hill – which is total proof that I continue to doubt myself all the time. After checking several sources, I found that this time we'd definitely been up the right hill, as confirmed by the explanation that the brick structure at the top appears to be an abandoned water reservoir. Then I checked YouTube and watched a couple of videos – just to confirm that, this time, we'd definitely reached the same hilltop as other adventurers.

I'm pleased to say we did.

Chapter Ten

HUNGRY HIKERS

On the Monday before this walk of the final Saturday of May, a heavy sense of sluggishness greeted me as I awoke. I elected to combat this with a cold shower, but instead of giving me a much-needed boost the freezing water hit me full-on, causing me to flinch and yell. My neck jolted and I strained my muscles as a result.

For the next few days, a triangle of pain throbbed between my neck and shoulder blades – causing sleeplessness and agitation – and, by midweek, I was properly suffering as lightning bolts of agony juddered down my spine. Any task I had to perform required a lot of pre-planning and slow movements; at times, it felt like an elephant had placed its huge behind on my neck as I bent down.

This whole debacle had seen me postpone my workouts and limit my footsteps to only those that were absolutely necessary. I became lethargic and grumpy, especially as we'd all been spurring each other on with our health drives. Aaron had completed a few Parkruns by this point, and his previous injuries were no longer causing him concern; Robert had also been continuing with his jogging efforts, racking up a spring half-marathon or two in the process; and Robin had been committed to after-work sojourns and the gym. For me, 'snackercise' had just turned into 'snack'!

One day over social media, Aaron mentioned the idea of having a cooked breakfast whilst we were in Scotland. Fry-ups are a staple of any holiday, but at that moment in time I was particularly glad to hear it – I needed comforting news.

Robin replied, 'That's how we'll roll in Fort William.'

'Hash browns, beans, mushrooms, waffles, sausages, bacon...these are just a few of my favourite things,' I responded.

'And beer!' Aaron added.

We were ready and primed – except me, due to being in gyp and generally acting like a cranky old git full of world-weary mistrust.

As the pain became more amplified, I started to reconsider going up Ben Nevis. Muscle heat rubs, hot water bottle treatments, self-massage, and ice packs: these tried and tested methods hadn't worked at all. Only when I wore a scarf for twenty-four hours (in balmy Spring weather) did the ache begin to dull. The spinal shudders continued until Friday afternoon when I took some painkillers, which I'd inexplicably not considered up to that point, and it was then that I made the decision to go.

By the time I'd given Robin absolute confirmation that I'd be able to make that weekend's escapade after all, a heavy concern had engulfed me as to whether I'd actually be able to get through this particular walk. Even if I didn't complete the whole route, however, I knew I needed to be out in the countryside; after being stuck inside for the best part of a week, I very much needed the fresh air.

Robin recommended heading out to the Chilterns in search of hills, and this time we chose to find our own route, relying on the GPS on our phones. We agreed that if I had to stop early, it would be fine. I'd hoped not to take my rucksack in order to reduce the strain on my back, yet due to heavy rain and thunder being a possibility, I needed something to store my waterproofs in.

We commenced at a pub in a village called Aston, before curving through a meadow that hugged the Thames. Yonder, the wooded hills offered tranquil viewing.

We soon crossed the river at a lock, noticing the increasing number of cyclists and hikers who were enjoying the unrelenting sun. At this sight, I nagged myself for putting the increased weight upon my poor back.

Through miraculously green fields we paced as we followed the meandering river up into the hills, the rush of the breeze through the shaded woodland providing some temporary escape from the afternoon sun as we crested the Iron Age Hill Fort site of Medmenham Hill, passing deer on the other side. We peered at the information boards explaining what everyday life had been like for our ancestors, and I wondered if they'd ever met the residents of Walbury Hill long ago.

At another village, and faced with a long path, we stretched out for a few minutes on a grass verge. I rummaged through my backpack and realised I'd forgotten to pack any food or drink, while Robin only had a small bottle of water. We checked the GPS for a nearby village store, a lack of which was confirmed by a passing dog walker, who kindly gave us directions to the nearest pub a mile away as the crow flies. But this was the pub we'd started at, and we agreed that to go back would be to admit defeat. So, with empty bellies and parched mouths, we marched defiantly on.

'I can see a pub about four miles east-ish of here,' Robin said, scanning the map on his phone.

'We'll aim for there, then.'

'And we need to take shade as well. There's a forest en route,' he added.

'Great – thanks, mate,' I replied hazily.

After all the appalling weather we'd put up with during our walks, we now had some sunshine, yet we were unable to enjoy it as we should have done.

'How come we're so underprepared?' I asked.

'Sometimes we just are. We've done walks so many times before that perhaps we take it for granted that we're going to be okay,' Robin answered, sounding rather contemplative.

'And because we think we're likely to come across a pub,' I pointed out.

We both nodded at this truism before approaching the forest Robin had spotted, and as it turned out, this was a Site of Specific Scientific Interest. Even though we knew we were the only people around – something we'd normally stop to appreciate in a place like this – we pushed on with just the pub in mind, only briefly basking in the light birdsong and the gentle wind as it blew through the trees. I listened out for the sound of running water – at this stage I'd have had no issue with glugging back mouthfuls from a stream – but there was no such luck today. We remarked, appreciatively, that the pathway through the forest had clear markings, and the respite the canopy provided from the sun boosted our spirits as we went.

Once out the other side of the forest, we crossed a road and blitzed along a winding path before hitting some seemingly never-ending sun-kissed farm fields. At this point, my mind blanked out and my legs took over; I'm not able to offer any explanation of the route we took as the search for sustenance became paramount.

Eventually we found the pub, which was situated in another timeless village somewhere, but their expensive menu didn't respect our restricted budgets. So, we necked back our pints in a beer garden that we could easily have spent more time in if our wallets had allowed, and after exiting the pub we finally found a corner shop and bought some pasties, thus marking the end of our poor attempts at extreme survival.

It was mid-afternoon now, and the whole day slowed down as we observed what a picturesque and beautiful place this was, whatever it was called. Stone houses with flowered front lawns framed a green on all sides, and families and couples lounged on the grass, licking ice creams or guzzling back fizzy drinks. Dogs chased after each other as their respective owners called them to heel, and cyclists dismounted to purchase a well-earned treat from the store.

'That's better,' Robin sighed as he took a generous bite from his pasty.

'Yeahhhhh!' I exhaled before promptly demolishing my snack.

After wiping down the crumbs, with a nod of our heads we decided to start the final leg, the pace becoming less intense now that our tummies were satisfied. For about 30 minutes we followed a stream through some fields, before going over the Thames by bridge once more to reach the pub in Aston that marked our starting point. Some pub chips would have been a good reward, but a wannabe mockney barman screwed up his face at us when we asked if they were still serving food.

'Chef packed up early,' he gruffed.

So, instead, we consoled ourselves with a coke and a fist bump. And some pork scratchings.

On the way home, I realised that my desire for food and drink had overridden any memories of back pain.

This hike provided plenty of hills over which to test our legs, and the variety of scenery brought home just how close we were to being able to have a great mini escape – even if the desire for food overrode our enjoyment at times.

The pork scratchings were a bonus, though.

Chapter Eleven

THE BIG WEEKEND

Not wanting to aggravate my neck, I decided to cut out my workouts until after Ben Nevis; instead, I limited myself to completing mammoth evening walks in order to maintain my fitness for the Scotland trip and, by the weekend before our ascent, I felt confident I'd be fit enough.

Not wishing to overdo it either, Robin had been doing lighter workouts than usual at the gym. Aaron, however, had shaken off his knee problem and had challenged Robert to a Parkrun in Fort William the very day after the hike! Just the idea of it made me feel knackered – and that was even before we'd set foot on Scottish soil.

All this moderately healthy thinking and living can be quite taxing, so to balance it all out we kept topping up the list of culprits that were going to appear on our breakfast plates the morning after our mountain tour. Black pudding, onion rings, garlic mushrooms…the meal would be as high as the mountain itself and, of course, washed down with a river of tea.

I'd watched many more videos of Ben Nevis, Fort William, and the Highlands in general to prepare for what lay ahead –

and because I was oozing with excitement as the big day got closer and closer. Said to be the 'adventure capital of Britain', Fort William features an outdoor pursuits centre, skiing, and endless walking opportunities to name just a few. Of course, we were only going to be there for a long weekend in early June, but this trip would stay etched in our hearts and memories forever.

In the run-up to our trip I also kept checking the Ben Nevis Webcam, keeping the guys updated about the weather via social media. Some days Ben Nevis hadn't even rolled out of bed, as the mountain was layered in dense cloud; other times, it stood dominant and proud in quiet solemnity. And, yes, whenever I saw it I would wave to the mountain as eagerness and the need for adventure encouraged me to make a new friend.

Travel Day

Robin, Robert and I slowly weaved our way to the pick-up point at Glasgow Airport. Although there'd been an initial buzz when Robert and I had met at Robin's house that morning, the monotony of hanging about at Gatwick and an uneventful plane journey had left us all feeling a bit flat.

As we quick-stepped to the Glasgow Airport car park, Aaron boosted our ebbing spirits by texting to say he'd be in a light blue hatchback – though this brief spike in mood dipped when we saw that his car was the same colour and model as every taxi we could see! After a few minutes of scanning this way and that, however, we finally managed to locate our fellow adventurer, who was waving at us enthusiastically amongst the long line of blue.

Having driven up from Yorkshire, Aaron had already been on the road for about five hours by the time he got to us, and after we got in the car he continued on to Fort William, adding another two and a half hours onto his driving time. The rest of us had used a variety of transport options to get to the pick-up point: car, foot, train, and plane. We'd so far been focusing more on getting there than the actual hike, but when Robert had picked me up that morning we'd agreed that our little expedition had finally become very real.

This air of excitement continued as we reached the city limits, leaving Glasgow for the compelling scenery that didn't abate even once as we made our way to Fort William. Soon, Loch Lomond came into view on our right, its dark marble surface reflecting the smoky grey clouds above. To our left, forests and open grassland sprawled out into the distance.

As we drove further north, the Trossachs hills – and then mountains, with clouds dancing and swirling at their peaks – framed this wonderful landscape. Occasionally we'd pass a pub, caravan park, or small settlement, whilst farmsteads with seemingly no access roads could be seen dotted high on the slopes.

This terrain was truly different to anywhere we'd walked that year, and as we drove through the spectacular scenery I wondered if we'd done enough to prepare ourselves for Ben Nevis. Robin tried to reassure me, stating that as long as we were of reasonable fitness, we'd be fine. Robert and Aaron both concurred as their main form of exercise had been jogging, and this had seen them conquer Scafell Pike and Snowdon. This grounded me, and soon Robert and Aaron were back to talking about family and work as Robin and I resumed our snack eating.

As we drove higher into the mountains I dozed in and out of sleep, drifting off to the songs on the radio, and at around 8 p.m. we arrived in Fort William – a hilly town with rows of streets stacked above each other overlooking Loch Linnhe. Robin had chosen the accommodation well: a modern open-plan holiday home that gave us privacy, comfort, and freedom. As we unpacked the car and dumped our bags, we all agreed that this would be the ideal base camp for our weekend expedition.

After choosing my room I flopped, star-shaped, onto the bed, the softness of the duvet almost lulling me straight to sleep. As I lay there for a few moments, however, I wondered how many other journeys up Ben Nevis this home had been a starting point for. How many memories were etched into its walls – memories that our own would soon join?

After a quick freshen up we headed downhill through a maze of streets and alleyways into the lively town centre for dinner and supplies. Pubs, gift shops, whisky specialists, and outdoor activity stores lined a high street that had the appeal of a thriving outpost lost in time – the final place to stock up before we took to the wilderness.

Fort William had been a hotbed of action in the shaping of British history ever since medieval times, as the English crown looked to assert itself in Scotland. Indeed, Oliver Cromwell had a wooden citadel built there in the mid-seventeenth century before a more permanent fort was built under King William III in 1698 (see how the town got its name?). Since the building of the latter structure, Fort William had been a focal point in such events as the Glencoe Massacre, the Highland Clearances, the Jacobite Rebellions, and the Disruption of the Church. Today, though, it's the place to come for those in search of adventure and good whisky.

Although little remains of the fort, there's a real charm to this historic town, and – had we been there longer – I'd have happily spent an afternoon in the local museum, delving deeper into its broad history.

The Big Day

At 7.30 a.m. a series of alarms echoed throughout the house and a collective sigh could be heard as several snooze buttons were tapped simultaneously. Several minutes later – at the second wave of our phones buzzing – we were all up, and I pulled up the heavy blind to see bright blue skies. Over on the other side of the loch the blue-grey mountains focused our minds for the task ahead as seagulls soared above the clear waters and the town slowly sparked into life.

After a quick breakfast, we travelled by car to the Ben Nevis Visitor Centre, getting there around 9 a.m. A quick scan of the car park – which was full of vehicles that had arrived before we did – suggested the Tourist Path would be chock-a-block, but we immediately realised that rather than being in the midst of a steady stampede, we were actually part of a moderate trickle as the groups and individuals ahead of us were dispersed along the path. I had a fleeting yearning for us to have the route to ourselves – having everything that lay ahead being for us and us alone would be the ultimate escape – but then I changed my mind, hoping we'd meet some life-enhancing characters that would give this trip a twist of comic exhilaration.

Along with food and water, we'd made sure to pack our jumpers and waterproofs, but on this fine day we stayed adorned in our t-shirts and shorts, blessed by decent weather. (It's worth noting here again, though, that going on any walk involving altitude should not be done lightly. Although we didn't use any of our bad weather gear, we were well prepared – and there's so much to be said for that.)

Soon after leaving the Visitor Centre area, we crossed over the River Ness on a wooden bridge that swayed from side to side under our collective weight and, right from the beginning, the clearly-routed path started to incline. The river ran through the basin of the Glen Nevis Valley, and as we passed a bunk-house and a farmstead, a deeper sense of wonderment energised me, causing me to gaze skyward at the lofty peaks.

Butterflies skittered and flowers jived as a light breeze provided a gentle relief. We walked on, the slope growing ever steeper.

'We'll be ready for Kilimanjaro in no time,' announced Robert.

'Hmmm, I'll need plenty of pasties for that one!' Robin remarked.

'Imagine it: higher than the highest peaks of England, Scotland, and Wales combined,' Robert added.

'One day…yeah, one day! That'd be the ultimate,' Robin agreed dreamily.

'If Wayne got hit by dizziness, he'd have to be carried up,' chuckled Aaron as he led from the front.

'That might be a problem if I've eaten too many pasties!' I replied, smiling.

We passed a group of German tourists making the ascent, then they passed us, and then we passed them again, this slingshot effect driving us on. We then noticed a set of charity hikers further ahead and pulled ourselves forward to play 'mutual catapult' with them. Such tactics were important in propelling us on; whilst the heart-stopping views intoxicated our senses, the steepening route ahead demanded the best from us, and such strategies were essential if we were to complete this awesome task.

Then it hit me: that dreaded fear-inducing vortex sensation overwhelmed my mind as everything started whizzing about me at cyclonic speed. This happened when we'd got about three or four hundred metres up, and when I looked down everything seemed far more miniscule than it had just moments before. Ahead, Big, Bad Ben Nevis seemed to have risen infinitely in height.

I kept my head down, focusing on my feet, though this tactic only worked for a few seconds at a time as eventually I'd need to look up again to see where I was walking. My legs were heavy, drained of vim, and – to make matters worse – giant blocky steps had now appeared on the course, requiring me to intensify my waning concentration. I attempted conversation, took deep breaths...but nothing seemed to be working. Eventually the angle of the path sharpened skyward and, much to my dismay – but knowing I had to be sensible about this – I asked the guys to stop by some boulders at the side of the path.

Sweat cascaded out of me and my t-shirt stuck to my skin as I began to overheat.

'Stop and drink some water,' Aaron demanded, noticing my sudden affliction. 'You should've said something earlier.'

I slumped onto a nearby rock and did a quick self-check. My body was screaming at me to keep going, telling me that all the walking and exercise I'd done in preparation would see me through; my mind, on the other hand, offered a much safer option, telling me to stay where I was until the others came back down.

Robert fixed me a look as if to say, 'You can do this'. Robin sacrificed his walking pole for me to use, and Aaron grabbed my rucksack from the floor, telling me he'd be carrying it for a while despite my protestations and apologies.

This wasn't how I'd envisaged being on this journey. I'd wanted to soak in the views, enjoy some interesting conversation, and notice how much my physical training had prepared me for the challenge. More than anything, I wanted to reach the top.

However, with renewed determination brought on by the support of my mates, I readied myself for the next stages. And that's what it became – stages – because I needed to stop maybe 10 or so times on the way up to steady my mind. This was necessary as, whenever I looked down, the effect was akin to the feeling of having my head plunged deep into cold water. The best remedy I found involved me closing my eyes, steadying myself for about 30 seconds or so, and talking myself up to reach the next break point.

Footstep by footstep, section by section, we progressed – even if it was at a far slower rate than we'd intended. My moans and apologies regarding our slow progress were always rebuffed by the others; the important thing, Aaron said, was that we were there and we were going to do this – no matter how long it took. The guys switched my bag between them as they batted away any attempt made by me to reclaim it.

Earlier in the day, I'd questioned Robin on the advantages of the walking pole. Now, though, I'd most definitely become a convert to its benefits: it acted like an extra leg to steady me as we gained height and as I sought out firm ground for my jelly legs.

Before too long, we found ourselves on a flatter stretch of path and, feeling the need to prove myself – even if only up to the start of the infamous zigzags – I led from the front with a quickstep, telling myself fitness would not be an issue today. To our left Loch Meall an t-Suidhe seemed to be inviting us in for a dip, tempting us even as we rose. As we hit the switchbacks, however, my legs gave out again.

As off-white clouds scuttered above and a train of tourists passed us, I just kept telling myself: Don't look too far down.

I remember thinking that the greys and greens of the slopes were far more grand and awesome than anywhere I'd ever been. I wanted to notice every contour, savour every scent, take in the fullness of the route – but any flicker of creativity immediately got beaten down by a frenzy of neurons bent on confronting all my anxieties.

We paused quite a few times on this stretch of the mountain, yet by now my mindset had changed: this clearly wasn't going to be an endurance-focussed mission, more a case of simply completing the task. As long as I finished, that was the only thing that mattered.

The steps became more pronounced, the landscape more craggy. The guys walked slightly ahead, offering encouragement, and every so often we'd break at each corner. I'd steady myself, stopping the head spins by shutting my eyes, and then build myself up for the next part.

I repeated this process until we cleared the zigzags, relieved and happy that I'd found a way of coping.

Now, as the surrounding peaks bunched together like knuckles on a giant's fist, the idea of actually reaching the summit seemed far more achievable.

Sitting on an outcrop of boulders, and with hardly a soul passing us at this point (maybe about a kilometre up), we drank in the complete and utter silence. It wasn't a sitting-at-home-the-only-sounds-being-the-clock-ticking-or-fridge-humming silence or a walking-in-town-at-night-the-only-sound-being-the-distant-sound-of-traffic silence, and it wasn't even the usual gentle symphonies nature provides. No, this was true silence: the whole of existence muted seemingly for our own pleasure.

I prayed then that that memory and that feeling would stay with me forever. There's true joy to be found in places that offer complete sanctuary from a highly frantic world.

I kept glancing at my feet, carefully placing the walking pole amongst the rock and scree to guide me, and soon we approached a snow field. I'd fallen behind the others a bit, and when I looked up from taking my baby steps I noticed Aaron making snow angels. He then ran back down the slope, sliding on his derriere – much to the amusement of the other walkers.

I'd followed the online guidance of carrying at least two litres of water, but now I found my supply had run out due to my profuse sweating. I'd have happily gobbled handfuls of snow to quench my ridiculous thirst, but doing so would have caused further dehydration and made my core temperature plummet. Fortunately, Aaron handed me a spare bottle he had and all was good again in the thirst department. In order to cool off a little, I settled for dropping to my knees and planting my face in the crisp white snow!

We passed several cairns that had been placed as waymarkers to mark the track, which would have been no use to me if I'd done this as a solo excursion; undoubtedly, with my dodgy sense of direction I'd have been set on a course to Dundee way before that point.

Even though the cloud had now become heavier, we managed to find our way up to the peak still wearing our shorts and t-shirts.

When we finally got there, the sense of jubilation we shared manifested itself into a group hug. We queued for a photo at the top of the cairn to make our conquering of Ben Nevis official, then we skirted around the weather station and other structures at the top, mindful of where we were stepping, being on such a rocky tabletop. I'd read that the top of the mountain was the size of two football pitches, but it seemed a lot wider and longer than that to me.

We settled close to the edge of the south side of the mountain, viewing the way we'd come and watching the climbers on the peaks opposite. From our lofty position we could see all of life before us, viewing all Creation like knackered gods who would soon descend back into the mortal realm.

As we munched our pasties in hungry unison, I noticed one guy standing in front of the cairn, trying to take the perfect selfie. Whenever somebody ascended the cairn he would tut at them and ask them to step down – which they did without complaint! This happened two or three times in his pursuit of a decent photo as he pouted and turned his phone this way and that. Once he'd completed this vanity project and relocated to another part of the peak for more shameless posing, people carried on queuing again as normal. It seemed he was more into himself than the intoxicating views around us.

As we started the return leg – with me carrying my own rucksack again – it became clear that the happier faces belonged to those going down Ben Nevis than those heading up. In that moment, I defied my anti-self-congratulation policy and applauded myself for being in the former group.

Heading down the zigzags, my legs began to lock as I leapt from one large rock-step to another. This was okay as long as I kept moving, and the walking pole kept me steady on the more uneven areas. Necessary breaks became fewer and shorter as I only needed the occasional quick stop to shut my eyes and steady my head from the distant views below.

Before we'd started our annual mountain walks, I thought that going down would be worse than going up because everything below would be right in front of me, giving me more concerns of falling from a great height. In fact, I've found it to be the other way round: going up is far worse whenever I look back or down. I'm not sure why; it just affects me that way.

(As I'm tapping this out on the keyboard I can see my hands beginning to glisten with sweat just thinking back to the ascent.)

The grassy slopes were blotted with scree and Robin attempted to slide down them in order to take some time off the journey. On seeing him lose his footing on the first attempt – and yet somehow regain his balance very swiftly – we decided this wasn't exactly the best approach.

After clearing the switchbacks and walking on a bit, we reached the stream to see other hikers filling their bottles. I don't think I've ever drunk quicker than I did that day.

Fully refreshed and stocked up on liquids, we carried on debating whether we should take a dip in Loch Meall an t-Suidhe, as it only involved a slight detour from the increasing throngs of afternoon hikers across some marshy grassland. In the end, Aaron proved the most courageous by going for a dip in a freezing lake that only came up to his waist.

The pathway would have been easier to negotiate if it wasn't for my legs locking each time I bounded off one of the giant steps.

The scenery was more fertile now, with lush grass and trees becoming the norm. I didn't envy those who were only a third of the way up, and by the time we crossed the swingy bridge at the bottom to buy a well-earned ice cream, I had no empathy at all (mostly because I was too bushwhacked to care).

We'd done it.

That night, we celebrated by having a curry in a Fort William restaurant that overlooked the loch. The food was delicious and the beer tasted far sweeter than usual. The establishment buzzed with holidaymakers and locals. However, we were content with nothing more than quiet nods of acknowledgement between munching the tasty fare on offer.

Afterwards, we ambled along the vibrant high street and found a small, dimly lit pub that was having an open mic night. Inside, we were greeted with whistles and claps accompanying an upbeat pace of guitar and violin as patrons showed their appreciation for the entertainment on offer: mesmerising and sometimes haunting Celtic music played for the pleasure of the locals and any travellers who strayed in from the night.

After ducking below the beams of the low ceiling, we perched on bar stools around a barrel and supped our pints, hemmed in by a bulging crowd. The warm burr of a Scottish accent here, the light and fancy tones of a French accent there...all around it became clear that the people – whoever they were and wherever they were from – were all up for having a good time.

The energy inside this place had a huge impact on our tired bodies and minds, refreshing them with such vigour that we were soon stomping and yelping along with the crowd to the frantic, edgy pace of the music. At this stage, I think if anybody would have asked us to hike Ben Nevis again, we'd have given it some serious consideration...maybe.

Between pints we exchanged tales with a retired American couple who were there on a biking holiday. We also attempted conversation with two French blokes, something that was rendered near impossible by the volume of the music and the swarm of voices around us. A few of the musicians who had done solo songs now formed the core of a freely-shifting ensemble that added new depths to the music: the fiddlers executed punchy trills, slides, and grace notes along to melodic or furious guitar strums as a couple of the players took turns on lead vocals.

As Aaron pitched up with another round, I looked at my three friends. In this moment, it felt good to be sharing this experience with them. It was just a great way to end what had been a truly fantastic day. Times like this need to be shared; they need to be remembered. And, sometimes, something so memorable happens to add to whatever you're doing that the whole thing becomes utterly unforgettable.

For there he was.

He'd always been there; we just hadn't noticed him.

He'd blended in well until now and, like a social viper, he'd found the exact right moment to strike.

Armed with a pint of iced water, a bespectacled, unassuming bald guy in his mid-fifties crafted a space between the crowd and the musicians – which was a heck of a feat in a pub that size – to form his own mosh pit. He jerked and darted about like he'd been attacked with a cattle prod, then slowed down into a flowing one-man Mexican wave before shaking himself into life once more. Each cycle lasted no more than a few seconds.

'What the…' said Robin, agape. 'Has my bank manager just walked in and gone mental in front of us?'

Aaron became the first to start laughing uncontrollably, while Robert struggled to swallow his drink. My stomach began to hurt as the giggles reverberated around my insides. Soon, even the slightest look at one another became enough to trigger the others off as we gawped at this vision of wonder before us.

The music got faster and he danced harder.

Then he sat down. Mid-song. Just in front of us.

'I was going to sit there,' he said to the French guys before he began playing air drums to the music.

The French guys shrugged.

'Who is this guy?' I asked.

'As I said, he's my bank manager,' chuckled Robin.

'You should talk to him,' Robert suggested.

Robin found this request tempting, but there's something to be gained purely from watching certain characters cut loose; sometimes, it's more enjoyable to simply observe.

'Leave him be,' I said to the others. 'Let him roam free.'

How the musicians kept straight faces as they performed I don't know; it must have been down to their ability to focus solely on playing, because by now there were a lot of guffaws and sniggers coming out of the crowd in appreciation of (or disbelief at?) this bloke. However, he was either oblivious or didn't care, especially when he lost himself in the more rapid sections of music.

Then the bank manager stood up and skirted around our table, before saying his farewells to a group of bemused women in their early twenties.

He returned to take a last gasp of water and then headed out, once more, into the night.

'Do you know him?' Aaron asked one of the women, thinking this man could be their university lecturer or a tutor of some sort.

'Never met him before,' she commented.

And with that we tipped our glasses towards each other in mutual acknowledgement of the amazing sight we'd just witnessed.

Soon we were racing up the hilly streets back to our holiday home, being carried on empty legs fuelled by curry and hysterical delirium.

The next morning, Aaron, Robert, and Robin completed the Parkrun in drizzly weather, and I didn't envy them one bit as I typed my journey notes up from the security of Aaron's car, buoyed on by the fact that a mammoth fry-up would be demolished by one and all upon our return to base camp.

That afternoon, we did much ambling around the charming Fort William, sampling free whisky in specialist shops, walking along a busy arterial road parallel to the loch, and trying battered haggis from a chippy. On returning to our Scottish abode that evening, we ordered take-away pizza.

It was then that I realised what this Ben Nevis weekend really was: the ultimate snackercise marathon.

Chapter Twelve

2019 WALKS

The winter of 2018-19 gave me time to reflect on how I could overcome my acrophobia, though I wasn't sure if seeking counselling to battle my phobia would be quite the right thing for me. After all, ever since 2016 I'd shown myself – year after year – that, despite going into panic mode every time I got to a certain point on a climb, I'd still be able to complete the intended course. So, instead, I decided to focus on mastering as many local hills as I could.

Our winter walks saw us take on the old stomping grounds of the hills around Pangbourne and Winter Hill, near Cookham in Berkshire: at 85 metres it might not appear to be the most obvious choice to help train for higher levels, but it's a steep hill from the off and it reminded me of some of the trickier parts of mountains we'd had to navigate previously. In 2017, Robin spent the odd day going up and down it five to 10 times as part of his fitness drive for Snowdon. Admittedly, I was a little less enthusiastic, doing it just the once before waiting at the top while he finished his chosen number of ascents.

As the beginning of 2019 dawned, we had no real design about the location for our big yearly adventure. Ideas circulated on our social media chat group about going back up to Scotland to attempt a section of the West Highland Way, or revisiting the Lake District, or even tackling a new British mountain range. It didn't need to be the highest point; it would just be good to spend some time together in the wilderness.

The idea of going abroad had never really come up between us, as up to that point we'd all been happy to make this an annual British adventure. There was Slieve Donard, the highest mountain in Northern Ireland, but Aaron had already done that himself and we wanted to go somewhere that would be new to all four of us.

'It's obvious, then,' Robin declared.

'Where?' we questioned.

'We'll go to the Republic of Ireland this year,' he answered. 'Carrauntoohil.'

Within a matter of minutes we'd all agreed.

It wasn't like the idea of going abroad didn't appeal; it was just a conversation that had never happened. Now, enthused by the idea of Ireland, we'd arranged our flights and accommodation (courtesy of Robin) within a couple of weeks.

When it came to my fitness I was now in a routine, having streamlined my workouts to a trio of five-minute sessions each day. This wasn't going to shift the pounds, but I found doing daily exercises in bite-sized chunks was a good motivator to keep consistent.

So, by the beginning of the first week in April I felt prepared when Robin explained that he'd organised a surprise ramble for the coming Saturday. All I had to do was be at his on the Friday night as we'd be setting off early the next morning.

'I need a good hour before I'm out the door in the morning,' I bemoaned as we supped our beers the night before this secret expedition.

'Well, we're leaving at 4 a.m. – up and out,' he confirmed.

'It'll still be dark then! Where are we going?'

'Wait and see. You can grab a couple of hours' kip in the car.'

Regardless of my bleary eyed protestations the following morning, we soon found ourselves hurtling up the M4 under the coffee-black sky to Mysteryville.

'Tea,' I chimed as Robin pulled into a service station somewhere near Bristol.

'We're nowhere near yet,' he pre-empted, before I could ask for the umpteenth time where we were headed.

I'd dozed a bit in the car, but I hadn't quite managed to go into full slumber mode, focusing instead on the views of the passing fields as they became clearer in the early morning light. As each junction passed I'd wondered if that would be our turning, but it never was.

Now, as we sat in a café swigging back the wake-up juice, Robin deflected my curiosity and focused instead on the day's football fixtures.

Back on the road again, we soon crossed the Severn Bridge into Wales.

'Is this a practice drive to Ireland?' I enquired, confused.

'Well, as we're flying to Ireland from Gatwick, no,' Robin answered. 'Nearly there now.'

We turned off the motorway onto country lanes, Robin quizzing me on the pronunciation of place names as we went; I'd been to university in Carmarthen, West Wales in the mid-nineties and had picked up a few random phrases here and there. I still watch the Welsh league football on S4C – the Welsh language channel – too, so I think my way of sounding out words is okay…more or less.

'Come on, where are we headed?' I pressed.

'What do you notice about the scenery?' Robin asked, grinning.

Underneath the industrial grey clouds, some increasingly steep hills had come into sight, and – trying to avoid the sensation of a pneumatic drill breaking through my chest – I'd begun to mentally prepare myself for doing something bigger than I'd imagined.

'Pen y Fan!' Robin finally revealed.

This was something extraordinarily bigger. I thought we'd be going somewhere quite hilly, but to do the highest mountain in South Wales (886 metres) caused my senses to immediately overload. However, instead of trying to opt out, I realised Robin had deliberately sprung this on me to help me face my fear head on.

'Okay, cool,' I said in as confident a tone as I could muster.

'You'll be fine. It's a good path up and I've got the walking poles,' Robin assured me.

It was 7 a.m. when we finally rocked up to the car park, and a few people were already ahead of us on the path.

The views of the valley were stunning. Sheep grazed silently in the fields, and high up on a remote country track sat a lone camper van; I pined for such a life, to live as permanently free as that.

'We're heading up this path,' Robin pointed out.

Ahead, the incline grew steep as he indicated the mountain, which lay beyond our current line of sight. My calm demeanour belied the fact that I was in a very ambivalent state: I wanted to do it and I was thankful to Robin for bringing me here, but what would happen if my head went halfway up and I became a gibbering fool from that point on?

As it turned out, however, this was the best I'd ever been on a mountain. Yes, it was steep – certainly, there was a scramble near the top – but this venue had an advantage over other mountains that I'd not experienced before: the valleys rolled upwards as we went, and so the drop below was never really big enough to make my head spin. It was a surreal experience, expecting my mind to turn over but it never quite happening – on the way up, I was calm and wary all at once.

Robin had certainly come up trumps, and I said as much; I appreciated the peace and beauty of the undulating deep green hills, as well as the fact that I could say hello to other hikers without looking like I'd keel over at any second. Another bonus was that we completed the climb in the time Robin said we would. For once, I was a sane human being hiking up a mountain!

Robin retold how he'd completed this splendid trek one dark November day the autumn before, and his foresight to return to this location had given me a wealth of confidence.

At the summit, the upper valley gleamed with a heavenly sheen as some cool air and a sit-down gave us the chance to recuperate amongst the other explorers. Several paths led between the mountains and across the fields, providing the chance for other adventures. Due to time constraints, however, we settled on conquering the neighbouring peak of Corn Du.

On the way back down we met a Californian couple who asked if we knew what bus would get them to the nearby town of Brecon. As we were headed that way, Robin offered them a lift, and as he drove we exchanged stories of mountain adventures – it was nice that I could offer mine in a positive state of mind.

After a full Welsh breakfast in the delightful town, we made our way back, and I reached home around 4.30 p.m. – meaning a total journey time of just over 12 hours.

What a trip! This had taken me right out of my comfort zone, and had been served with a side of 'surprise!' It was such a bonus to have completed this and it gave me such a confidence boost for the peaks of Eire.

In the aftermath of this day trip, I felt as if something had been unlocked within me, and we discussed other ways to make our hikes more novel. So, between our Pen y Fan hike and going to Ireland – which would, more or less, mark a year to the day of us conquering Ben Nevis – we created a mini hit list of achievable aims.

The first idea was easy, as Robin and I had discussed it before: we'd walk further than we'd ever done before on a day out.

This was completed a few weeks after the Pen y Fan trip. We roved along the towpath of the Kennet and Avon from Reading to Newbury, setting a new record of 20 miles and outstripping our previous personal best by three. Sure, people have walked further in a day, but this was our record. Although there were no hills on this course, the heaviness in my legs afterwards underlined the fact that distance walking is good preparation for mountains.

Then, on a nice sunny day in the middle of May, we packed up a disposable barbecue – along with burgers and sausages – and headed out to the picturesque village of Hampstead Norreys in West Berkshire. The quest to find a potential place to eat added another layer to the excursion; farm fields or riverside venues were considered until we arrived at a small woodland. Here we stepped off the main track into a small clearing, the circle of thick trees giving us protection from nosey parkers intent on destroying our fun.

Gorging on sizzling burgers, guzzling back cola in the open air, climbing trees, and pretending to be astronauts all provided great fun before we headed back to the real world. We also found a sign that said 'Private Woods' and an empty shotgun cartridge on the woodland floor, causing us to feel rather wary until we stepped out into a country lane and made our way back to the car.

This trip wasn't about hills, mountains, or distances. We weren't out in the deep wilderness trying to cut it as extreme survivalists. What we were doing was cultivating a new way to enjoy the outdoors. To keep fit, and to have fun. Even though we hadn't clocked up the miles, creating a positive state of mind was a good motivator.

Around this time I began to explore acrophobia as a condition a lot more. Up until then, looking at videos of the mountains I'd be tackling offered me a way to prepare/scare the life out of myself beforehand. Why I hadn't decided to look up acrophobia before this is again best explained by the fact that the obvious solutions can elude me for a good while before I finally think of them.

The research I did into dealing with acrophobia on hills and mountains is covered in a bit more detail later on, but around this time – yet again – I considered counselling for my phobia. After some reflection, however, I decided that Dr YouTube would serve me just as well, and I elected to watch as many videos as I could about people overcoming their fear of heights.

Seeing different people peering over the edges of cliffs or tiptoeing across a canyon on a tightrope caused my toes to curl, my palms to sweat, and my mind to go into a vacuum. I noted that my fear of heights only kicked in a few hundred metres up, so to see some poor people standing on chairs, fretting away, reassured me that my level of fear wasn't as extreme as some – though my heart went out to them and their debilitating conditions. Indeed, even if the only way I could deal with the view from the roof of a multi-storey building was to lie down and slowly poke my head over the side, it was important for me to acknowledge that I *could* face my fear, considering it wasn't as far along the spectrum as I'd thought.

Two overarching themes struck me when watching these videos: the symptoms and experiences of acrophobia are different for everybody, and even if the phobia is dealt with by methods such as counselling or virtual reality exposure training, it may never completely go away…it will just become more manageable.

All this self-reflection and research gifted me a deeper sense of focus for the impending Irish visit. I knew that, despite the tenseness and nervous anticipation that had filled my boots on every previous mountain, I had completed them thanks to the support from my friends and addressing my fears. Plus, my self-belief had now been reinforced by the Pen y Fan trip.

Keen to carry on at a higher level, I suggested to Robin that we visit Leith Hill, the highest point in Surrey at 294 metres. He agreed, and we chose to carve out a route reliant on our phone maps and a general sense of direction.

So, departing from Dorking station in the early morning sun on the final Saturday of May, we marched up out of the town centre onto hilly country lanes. Groups of cyclists flew past us both ways as we clung close to the edge of the tarmac to avoid an accident. Up we rose, and soon the outskirts of the town were behind us, a quilt of open fields overlooking the valley bowl coming into sight. We stepped off the tarmac and onto waymarked paths winding through the fields.

Once or twice we became confused about which way to go; however, the tower perched atop the hill we were aiming for would appear on the horizon periodically, giving us a general sense of direction. Soon we found ourselves in a deep forest, the track climbing up and up. Even if my mind didn't feel tested by the heights, this was definitely proving to be a good walk before Carrauntoohil in Ireland.

At one point a lady in a car passed us, turned back, and then asked us for directions to the hill. We said it was pretty much in the direction we were headed, but advised her that she'd only be able to access the hilltop by foot from this side. She thanked us and drove away. The next minute she passed us again, seemingly determined to defy our instruction. We passed her yet again as the path narrowed further on, her teenage son directing her back up the pathway to find a place to turn around.

'Glad I didn't drive today,' Robin quipped.

Leith Hill is on National Trust land and does have car parks, just not on the path we were travelling along. As I watched the woman drive past yet again, I thought to myself that perhaps my sense of direction and general travel skills weren't altogether that bad.

The passage became steeper and steeper, and finally we saw the signs for the hill.

Climbing out of the forest, we took in the expansive views below as we reached the apex of the hill – which was littered with families, dog walkers, and cyclists.

Scouring around for a spot to rest our weary pegs, Robin espied the entrance to the tower. Inside, I clung onto a rail that led up the spiral staircase, looking ahead for any shafts of light piercing through the darkness. We got to the top, and from the roof of the tower we enjoyed all that was sprawled before us: towns and villages were dotted about in clusters, faraway vehicles were seemingly being pulled along as if by the hand of an invisible child, and further out, planes were ascending into the sky from Gatwick Airport. I crept back down the staircase, the torch on my phone guiding me as I nervously made my way downwards. I'd forgotten how spun-out I can get on spiral staircases!

When we were ready, we followed the path out the other side and down the country lane to the train station, being wary to stand clear of any cyclists who bombarded past us without due regard. This had been a varied walk, and on the way back I reflected to Robin that, although I'd not conquered many heights, the fact that I'd done so well on Pen Y Fan had given me the confidence I needed for the Irish trip.

So, to find myself self-cussing again as I descended the narrow path of the adjacent mountain to Carrauntoohil two weeks later caused fear and despair to fill my body, permeating to my very core while arrows of rain and driven winds plagued us all the way down.

I'd started the day feeling as bright as the others as we alighted from the car. We'd navigated the stony track before venturing onto the rockier terrain that meandered through and next to a river, the streams that flowed into it blending into the rugged greens and greys of the mountains. Then we clambered over rocks before taking on the infamous Devil's Ladder which, as Robin pointed out, was somewhere between a scramble and a climb.

I took the front as I was concerned that, had I been anywhere else in line, I'd have slowed everybody down; going first meant that I had a greater reason not to time-waste. The climb was a good hundred metres or so, and the extra responsibility took my mind away from the possibility of my acrophobia kicking in.

It was only when I looked down from the top of the ladder that I could sense my brain turning over; to trek back down that way would have been a constant cause of tremors in my body.

'We'll be going down that way,' said Aaron, pointing to the location of our return journey – not the direction I'd been looking in.

A sweet symphony played in my ears at these words and I continued to the scree mound that marked the way to the peak, where we were joined by a jovial Austrian bloke who kept offering us sweets. After taking photos, I sat a while to focus on the return leg whilst Aaron, Robin, and Robert scouted the perimeter. Up until now the day had been still and grey. Now, though, thick, ugly, smoke-coloured cloud began to roll over and a cloak of mist played havoc with the visibility.

We hotfooted the distance between Carrauntoohil and the next peak, and as we did so I silently congratulated myself that I'd made it this far without my usual whining. Was I finally ridding myself of my affliction?

Alas, and oh dear, I was struck by the curse of being over-confident too soon.

As we headed along the sawtooth top line of the mountain, the rain and wind lashed against us and my ego nosedived as I peered down to the valley floor far, far below.

I trembled with every step, the others taking turns to stay back and support me. Soon, though, I was falling way behind and the deluge showed no sign of abating. Down below, sharp rocks took on the form of shark fins or dragon's teeth.

About halfway along a couple passed me in relative calm, striding purposefully, and I saw the others resting on an outcrop of rock. In hastening my step I tumbled forward, stood up, and instantly went over again. Thankfully, this path was way wider than before, so I was spared from going headlong downwards.

From here on in I calmed down, as the riverbed at the bottom became a more comfortable distance below. Between these two points I began to breathe more steadily, and I was even able to skip over the rocks at the bottom. I'd wanted to lead from the front again, but I felt emotionally beaten – at least, until we made it to the pub that night.

Killarney, the nearest tourist town to the mountain range, is an attractive place where locals and tourists intermingle seamlessly. In one pub-club we were treated to fast-paced Celtic music and Irish dancing – the broom dance being the standout moment – followed by a few live bands and a disco. When we left this establishment in the early hours, my legs experienced no lethargy on the 40-minute walk back to our holiday home, possibly because they'd warmed up thoroughly with a beer-fuelled workout on the dance floor.

The Irish people we spoke to were warm and accommodating: we enjoyed having the rules of Gaelic football explained to us, were enthralled by the game on the screen, and were offered fair counsel to stay away from sampling the infamous Poitin, and to instead partake of the Baby Guinness. Robin and Robert noted from the locals that tackling Carrauntoohil was more of a tourist thing – a few locals had been perplexed that this was our main reason for visiting – but we agreed that the opinion had only been formed from the few people we'd spoken to.

Ireland left us with a lot of great memories and, for a good couple of weeks after, sadness lingered with us about leaving Killarney behind. Aaron provided the tonic sometime after, however, when he announced that we should attempt the Yorkshire Three Peaks.

I agreed instantly, noting how much I'd changed: previously, after having just completed a mountain, I'd have declined another climbing offer like a hysteric basket case. Yet now here I was, ready to continue confronting my anxieties.

Aaron suggested a date for mid-October, and in preparation, Robin and I committed to doing distance walks. The Yorkshire Three Peaks course we'd be taking was a little under 25 miles, and the motivation of smashing our personal bests for mountains hiked in a year – and length covered on a single walk – heightened our desire to keep going.

When we started hiking as a hobby, it was all about being out in the fresh, open air, clearing our heads of the stresses of daily life. So much had come from those first steps, and to have a deeper sense of self by confronting a phobia and pushing through set goals fuelled me to go outside more and more. Primarily, though, it was the search for jaw-dropping scenery and tranquillity that ignited my interest.

The Yorkshire Three Peaks includes Pen-y-Ghent (694 metres), Whernside (736 metres) and Ingleborough (723 metres), and we tackled the mountains in that order, starting out from our campsite at 7 a.m. We estimated that it would take us 11, maybe 12 hours, but by the time we actually completed the route it was more like 15 and a half.

The conditions were decent for the time of year; a slight drizzle had greeted us as we set off, then clear skies moved in. I coped well, and the elation I felt when leading from the front on several occasions gave me the confidence to know I wouldn't hold the others back. A few scrambles here, a few scrambles there...sometimes a long view down caused me to stay focused on the path ahead, but mostly the valleys climbed up alongside us and we enjoyed progressing through them as we appreciated the open moors. For once, I found myself able to actually contribute to the banter rather than having a conflicted state of mind.

At Ingleborough a climb akin to the Devil's Ladder greeted us, and taking the lead again I scampered up, refusing to look down.

'You did this in Ireland, you can do this now,' I told myself.

Fortunately, Aaron did such a grand job of distracting me from my fear with talk of the latest sci-fi shows we'd been watching that we found ourselves at the top of the climb in good time. The sense of elation was short-lived, however, as a spectral twilight had kicked in and we steeled ourselves to get to the peak and make the descent before nightfall ground us to a halt.

After a while the darkness became impenetrable, but thankfully we'd brought torches with us – we certainly hadn't underestimated this challenge.

With heavy legs and the terrain constantly altering between rock-steps, with churned mud and waterlogged paths, we soon became lost. Retracing our steps through boggy fields that tried to swallow us wasn't fun, and our phones were out of range and slow to work. The awesome scenery now had a menacing quality to it, but after getting back on the right path, we steeled ourselves for the remainder of the journey.

Robin pointed to the village lights, that last mile somehow seeming to double the total time of the entire trip.

Aaron phoned ahead to the pub to order food, and although we gave an estimated time of arrival, we ended up getting there much later.

With fear of trench foot adding to our woes, we finally arrived, much to the bemusement of other patrons who'd finished hours before. We had our dinner in near silence before returning to the campsite for a nightcap and some much-needed sleep.

After waving Aaron off the next morning, Robin drove us back to Berkshire. That weekend I'd introduced him to a pastime Aaron had initiated me in some years before during a long car journey: Eddie Stobart lorry spotting! My previous record for any journey was nine. On the journey up to Yorkshire we'd hammered that, increasing the record to 15, whereas the return journey saw us spot 23 (I don't include the time when, on a journey with another mate through Burton-on-Trent, I passed an Eddie Stobart depot that was chock-full of trucks – this served as a bonus level to an eternal pursuit).

Although we were dozy eyed, we enthused about the possibility of our next destination. Between us, we'd previously agreed that we'd shut down our big walks in November every year due to the early darkness and the inevitable change in weather that month brought with it. That would bring a three or four-month hiatus – unless we were able to sneak in a few good weather winter walks – and so by the time February or March came we were always like dogs pulling their owners along, wanting to run free in the park.

This next tour, we decided, had to be testing while also offering us the chance of a good escape if the conditions changed, so the next day I looked at an atlas and pored through the pages of the southern half of England. I scanned each county in turn, a buzz of anticipation enveloping me as I took in all the options. Cornwall offered rugged beauty, Devon gave the chance to experience some peaceful isolation, Kent was a county little explored by me...each one had its own merits. The shivers of joy I experienced whenever planning a hike always guided me to discovering new locations.

I nodded approvingly as I considered Worcestershire, and more specifically the Malvern Hills. After looking at more maps of the area it was clear that there were well-defined routes snaking all over the hills that would offer numerous passages to sanctuary, should we require it. The entire walk consisted of nine miles south to north over a decent number of hills, the highest of which was Worcestershire Beacon at 420 metres. As the higher peaks were on the north side we could build ourselves up to taking them on in the afternoon.

Robin agreed straight away but, unfortunately, Robert and Aaron were unable to make the trip.

Despite the photos I'd seen of the countryside surrounding the Malverns, there were no such views on offer that day as we were contained by an increasingly dense fog and heavy rain; by the time early afternoon hit the visibility was no more than 30 or 40 metres. We'd underestimated the amount of time it would take us to have an extra beer at lunchtime, so as night-time and the heavy fog shrouded us, our torches were the only way to find a clear path ahead on tracks that were often marshy. At least the Yorkshire Three Peaks had given us the wisdom to pack correctly for this trip.

We'd been craving the warmth of the hotel since early on in the slog, and so, once we'd finished our hike and returned to the bar, we savoured the first taste of evening beer.

After a mediocre night's sleep due to pipes banging all through the night, I awoke and we headed to a café. Here I was confronted by an uptight owner, who attempted to berate me for selecting ketchup with my Full English.

'Nobody has red sauce after the age of eight,' he concluded with his pseudo banter.

'It's a matter of preference,' I shrugged.

Whenever subsequent patrons stated their preference for brown sauce, he would look over at me with a frown. I just shrugged some more. I did a moderate amount of shrugging over that breakfast, and I think I was becoming quite good at it: sometimes I'd do it with arms outstretched and open palms, and other times it would be a quick lift of the shoulders with or without a cursory glance. The art of shrugging is severely under-estimated.

To round it all off, we only spotted one Eddie Stobart lorry on the way back to Berkshire.

Sadly, the Malvern experience hadn't enthralled us as we'd needed it to. However, we both agreed that the area was worth another shot on a sunny weekend, both in terms of the scenery and unintentionally winding up café owners about having ketchup on scrambled eggs.

With that, 2019's offerings were complete. We'd done a lot, seen a lot, and had tested ourselves so much more than ever before. I'd become more accustomed to facing my acrophobia and, although I knew it would no doubt rear its ugly head from time to time, I also knew it wouldn't stop me experiencing the kinds of adventures we sought.

Whilst this self-knowledge will provide the basis for being bolder in the wilderness, I'm always acutely aware that if anxiety throttles the sanity out of me on a hike, that's when I'll stop.

Having good friends to share these adventures with adds new depths to who we are, both individually and collectively. When the day comes to hang up the walking boots – and let's hope that won't be for a long time yet – it will be great to look back and trace all these wonderful memories.

Chapter Thirteen

2020 PART ONE

As 2019 drew to a close I was optimistic about the progress I'd made in overcoming my acrophobia. The lessons I'd learnt and the ways in which I'd tested myself had given me a big dose of self-esteem – not to mention a more established skill set. As we discussed possible destinations for 2020 to carry on with our expeditions, Northern Ireland rose up again as a viable option. A trip to the Shetlands or Orkneys also sounded enticing, while Aaron offered the idea of Bosnia to take our adventuring even further afield.

Then it happened: things began to slow down – and then seemingly stopped completely – all across the world as the Coronavirus stamped its nefarious authority on the lives of millions of people.

2020 will be remembered by everyone as a crazy, crazy year. While many families very sadly lost loved ones to the devastating sickness, we also had to contend with the impact of Covid-19 in other ways: economies and health systems became fragile; our mental health needs became precious; and life became...well...

far more rubbish. We all found ourselves with new and different mountains to climb, both individually and collectively.

Over the next three chapters, I'll recount how I adapted my hiking pursuits and mountain training throughout that strange, scary year, though – as this is primarily a book about hiking – I'll only briefly touch upon Covid-19 information where appropriate. Instead, my primary focus will be on how I adapted my practices to keep my spirit for adventure alive.

In fact, I believe hiking was one of the main factors that enabled me to navigate through what was, for all of us, such a tough, brutal year.

January to March (Pre-Lockdown)

January provided me with the opportunity to have a few local, brisk walks, despite the cold weather; I remember going on one such hike and loving the feeling of being wrapped up under heavy layers, protecting myself against the chill. Plus, it makes you feel more hardy as you embrace all kinds of weather.

February brought with it Storms Ciara and Dennis so, therefore, there were fewer chances to walk; still, home workouts compensated in the interim. As the storms died out, though, Covid-19 was growing in stature – and so was talk of a national lockdown.

Towards the end of February, I met Robin in London for one of our city winter walks. For a while we'd been considering going to the Imperial War Museum to understand more about the conflicts of the last century, so we took the opportunity to visit it while we were in the capital. It was a very sobering experience – the Auschwitz exhibition will certainly live with me for a long time – and we appreciated the great many sacrifices made by others so that we may be able to follow our own pursuits in the present day.

Like many people we overheard talking that day, a lot of our conversations were to do with the growing concerns presented by the virus. We just hoped that, if we went into lockdown, it wouldn't be too long before we'd be back out again.

Lockdown One, Part One – March 23rd to End of April: New Hiking Hobbies

Then, on March 23rd, we went into full lockdown and everything changed. *Everything*. Everyone was scared and everyone felt incredibly uncertain about the future.

I remember thinking to myself early on how one of our tactics to get through the harder walks had been to pretend we were marching away from infected zombies, but now we had to stay at home in an attempt to prevent a deadly virus from spreading.

From the start, it was apparent to me that I'd have to limit my time outside to essential travel only, such as running errands for shielding family members. And, soon, it became clear to me that being indoors was the new outdoors.

From watching news articles and speaking with family and friends, it was also clear that we were all struggling to find new ways to cope. Being an outdoorsy sort, I knew I needed to adapt. The strange thing was, I was experiencing a kind of underlying anxiety that compelled me to want to stay in more –

regardless of whether it was the right thing to do – which was a completely alien feeling to me. I knew that, in order to get over my particular range of mental mountains, I'd have to navigate the foothills of emotion first.

A few times I completed 10,000 steps in my back garden, even to the point where I packed a snack and took a drink with me to simulate a hike as much as possible, feeling grateful that I had such a space to enjoy.

I felt a bit odd about doing this at first – especially in view of the neighbours – and so some mornings I'd wake up early to achieve my steps before anyone else was likely to be up. After several attempts, though, I became less inhibited and started completing the task any time of the day. This genuinely became a relaxing experience for me.

This led me to consider how I could complete my hikes indoors. Workouts were fun, but being stuck inside more meant I craved more variety to keep me fit.

But hiking indoors isn't hiking...is it?

I proffered this to the guys one night in mid-April when we were doing a group video chat. Pete (our mate who joined Robin and I for our very first walk to what we thought was Walbury Hill) was on hand to offer a solution.

'Do a virtual hike,' he said.

'What's that when it's at home?' I asked.

'Get onto YouTube, then type in the name of any random country you like, along with the phrase 'virtual walk',' he replied.

I hadn't thought of doing this, but it certainly seemed interesting.

The very next morning saw me pounding along a trek in the Swiss Alps. The sky was a crisp, sea blue, and the powder-coated mountains gave off an alluring sense of majesty. Then the kettle boiled and I was reminded that I was in my kitchen staring at the hiking video on my phone.

After a big gulp of tea, I proceeded along a gravel track that had the strange sensation of cold kitchen lino against my feet. Imagining that you're taking in deep breaths of cool alpine air is difficult when your nostrils are hit with a waft of toast, but this experience was definitely a welcome addition to my fitness endeavours.

Pete was right: there's a plethora of hiking videos shot in the first person on YouTube that cover many different countries. Whilst I think these may be more for people using treadmills, there's no harm in watching these while walking from room to room of your home, completing your step count at the same time. There are national parks, cities, and famous tourist attractions to name just a few. Sometimes the person walking would act as a tour guide as well, so I'd also be able to gain some knowledge of the place I was 'visiting'.

I really enjoyed exploring the world in this way, and was keen to develop this new interest further. It certainly encouraged me to stop taking to the sofa for extended periods of time and, sometimes, I'd even get up in the early hours to go for a walk around a national park in Canada or go on a street walk in Japan.

The big thing for me was that I noticed how my thoughts would unwind as if I was on a real hike. Sure, one second you're staring at a screen and the next you're looking out your window to see the bin crew collecting your rubbish, but these virtual hikes were as close as I could get to being properly in the world and, more importantly, the wilderness. It was still an escape, even if it was a virtual one.

After a few weeks I noticed that the anxiety I'd felt whenever I'd been outside in lockdown was easing, and I really believe that the various scenery I'd encountered on the virtual hikes played a strong part in that.

During another video chat in late April, I reflected to the others how I'd taken to this whole video hiking thing, acknowledging Pete's influence on my new hobby.

'It's funny,' mused Robin. 'One moment we're fleeing the imaginary undead to help us complete walks. The next we're having to stay inside to keep away from a real infection.'

I nodded, having had the same thought at the start of lockdown.

'It's important to go out, but it's also important to stay safe,' reflected Robert.

'It's like the world has reset itself and we're having to find new ways to cope,' said Aaron.

'I wonder when we'll be able to go to other parts of the UK,' I pondered.

'I think we've just got to stay local at the moment,' Robert said.

'Don't go mad, go local,' offered Robin.

Their words left an imprint on me, and I began to experiment with 'safer' routes to the ones I'd normally take as I started venturing outside a bit more regularly.

For one thing, I took longer journeys on roads I knew wouldn't be busy. In regular times, if somebody walked past you on a thin stretch of pavement, then either of you might step aside to let the other pass; in this day and age, though, I often found myself walking straight down the middle of the road to avoid walking past people altogether. In some ways it reminded me of being on quiet country lanes, as there was far less activity on the roads.

Going outside again required confidence. The important thing for me was just to be steadfast in going out for brief periods of time a few days a week (while staying socially distanced, of course) because the moment I thought otherwise and wanted to stay in, I knew I wouldn't be helping myself at all.

The main blessing at this time was that I found new streets in my town, streets that were even a little bit hilly! So, I incorporated those into my walks as much as possible. Even if everything was scaled down for the time being – where and how far we could go, and how long for – I appreciated that, by simply using a little imagination, I could immerse myself in the usual, familiar feelings of being on a hike. I was able to discover new places and get at least some kind of sense of the slopes I craved; plus, the more I was outside, the less anxious I became.

It was also during the first few months of Lockdown Part One that I looked at other new hiking-related hobbies, the catalyst for this being not knowing how long it would take pubs or cafés to open up – and how long they'd be open for – once the current restrictions eased.

I'd read a few books by adventurers who would head out into the wilderness and wild camp, and now the need to be out in the open and away from civilisation seemed more important than ever before. Reading turned into viewing and soon I was watching YouTubers who would (even just for the day) head off into the woods and cook meals from scratch. Some would build their own ovens with rocks and firewood they'd gathered from the forest floor; others might test out their latest camping stove and cookware. (If this interests you, then please see the handy tips at the end of this chapter and the Appendix for some basic advice).

Inspired by this, I experimented with building small safe fires (with eco-friendly firestarters) in my back garden and attempting to cook. At first, I was a bit chaotic in my approach; I found myself marching between my garden and my kitchen multiple times, having forgotten certain items. But soon I surprised myself with knocking up mini fry-ups or noodle soups – just simple things to boost my confidence. Simultaneously, I found myself becoming mesmerised by the orange-gold flame-like ribbons as they danced and twirled about. Even though my time out in the natural world was limited for now, here I was connecting with the elements on a deeper level. It became quite the fulfilling project to fill my time.

I mentioned this to Robin one evening on the phone.

'We could try that. I've got a little camping stove I could bring along.'

'That's a good idea,' I replied. 'I wouldn't want to start a fire in the woods in case it got out of control.'

'Yeah, plus, making a fire would probably draw attention to us,' highlighted Robin. 'They're probably best used in really remote areas, and only in an emergency. Still, it's a handy skill to have.'

'It's quite hypnotic watching a fire. Quite relaxing, really,' I told him.

'There are campsites that allow fires. Or maybe we can look at doing wild camps in the future,' added Robin, nodding.

'We're becoming a bit more self-sufficient in the great outdoors,' I remarked.

Despite having spent more time inside, I felt as though this year was preparing me for more adventures in times ahead – and with added layers thanks to all these new skills I was learning. How great it would be to share them with my mates! Even the idea of boiling up a brew in the middle of the woods or by a river and appreciating where we were in the moment sounded both satisfying and enriching. Again, I reflected how hiking had given us so much: more side hobbies and skills that we could incorporate into our adventures to make them more memorable.

During our video calls over the first few months of the original lockdown, we chatted about the different ways we'd been keeping fit. Robert had continued to jog, choosing to find a ton of new courses around his area. Living near the countryside,

Aaron had spent more and more time exploring the outdoors, carving out new, local adventures. Robin, too, had made extra use of his local area, especially the forest near to him; he said he'd hardly ever been there before, and he didn't know why he hadn't made more use of it previously.

We all took a moment to reflect on how much we hadn't known about our local surroundings until this year. The world had appeared to shrink, but our hometowns seemed so much bigger.

Lockdown One, Part Two: May to June – On Yer Bike For A Hike With New Items In Yer Kit

Into May and June, infection rates began to slow down; we were well past the first peak of the virus. As we hoped the lockdown would end soon, I thought to myself that this was the time of year we'd normally be doing our annual mountain challenge. As if on cue, my body seemed to start nudging my mind to take on greater feats.

I hadn't become bored with my virtual hikes – on the contrary, these had now become the centre-point of my fitness regime – it's just that I'm a member of a species that isn't used to being stuck inside for extended periods of time. I crave an assortment of hobbies, and coming up with novel ideas to keep me motivated was a constant struggle.

I encouraged myself by vowing to never go back to how I used to be in my pre-hiking days (even if I still enjoyed tucking into the odd Pot Noodle).

Then, one evening towards the end of that month, I paused the walking tour video of Ueno Park in Japan I'd been marching along to and noticed a suggested video for a virtual cycling tour. I watched it for a bit and it got me thinking.

With hiking I can see the world unfurl at a natural pace: plodding along and taking my time is a great way to enjoy the outdoors. Anything that's a bit faster than putting one foot in front of the other seems, to me, to be too quick a pastime to enjoy the world around me. However, this year had thrown a real curveball at us all – changing our worldviews and how we carry out our daily lives – so I was willing to turn my perspective of outdoor pursuits on its head in an attempt to stave off the boredom.

After a bit of a search I found just what I was looking for: a very cheap pedal exerciser. These portable, fold-up contraptions consist of a frame with two pedals either side and are roughly half a metre high. Perfect for using whilst sitting on the sofa, I reasoned this would be my perfect ally to explore the virtual world some more whilst confusing my mind into thinking I was having a rest.

Soon I was whizzing through the Alps, bolting along Iceland's Ring Road, and taking on any number of high-paced challenges. With the natural soundtrack and scenery already provided via the chosen video, I used my senses to imagine the aromas and the sensations of sunlight, wind, and rain, making it a truly immersive experience. Soon I was mixing up the cycling and the hiking, enjoying the thrill of new places; the more mountainous the scenery, the better.

But why stop there?

Next I sought out videos of the polar regions – hiking through Antarctica was a crazy and amazing trek – and biked seas and rivers as if I was on a pedalo. It was so fun to be pedalling around museums that I've now added several of them to my list of places I'd like to visit in real life.

I also enjoyed the aspect of confusing my senses with all of this, for here I was exploring the globe from the comfort of my front room and kitchen, conjuring up smells and sensations whilst at the same time listening out for the post to plop on the doormat. All this added to the spontaneity of my virtual visits.

Although I wasn't really there, I felt connected to the world on a more intimate level, and I knew that – even in a post-Coronavirus world – I'd carry on with this new hobby. There's also the added bonus of seeing that you're covering ground as you're exercising; doing regular workouts against the clock is great, but being able to enjoy the varied scenery as I pummelled it up and down hillside tracks became more and more appealing.

This gave me more confidence and a renewed vigour to explore the countryside again. Still, I felt that I needed to give much thought on how to be safe outside. For now, at least, hiking safely would need a rethink.

Being safe didn't just mean having the right equipment and being prepared for unexpected emergencies. Now, more items would need to be added to the kit list in order for me to stay safe. For this, I did some research on staying safe in open spaces during the pandemic, finding The British Mountaineering Council's advice in their Covid-19 poster to be both adequate and practical for our needs. Some of the advice concerned things we'd already grown used to (such as handwashing and social distancing, for instance), whilst other nuggets of wisdom included making sure that hikers are adequately supplied for walks as local shops may be shut, and to make sure that the area we're visiting could cope with an influx of visitors. Emphasis was also placed on respect: being considerate of locals, other hikers and rescue teams that might already be short on numbers.

Although it's not my intention to debate how long Coronavirus could last on surfaces, this was a question that was certainly on my mind given that we might need to use public transport, and gates and stiles, when out and about (I found a handy article in *The Great Outdoors* magazine, and I've included the link to it in the Appendix). The truth was, whilst I didn't want to get carried away with a sense of paranoia that would take away my enjoyment of being outdoors, I did want to carry on with my hobby in relative safety. Life had to carry on – it needed to – but being more practical and aware, at least for now, was definitely part of the zeitgeist.

With all this in mind I added the following, along with the necessary hand sanitiser and face mask, to my kit list: soap sheets and an extra bottle of water (to wash extra muddy hands in an emergency), paper towels, and disposable gloves (again, these suggestions have been added into the kit list in the Appendix). In addition to these, the mini camping stove, food, and utensils would periodically make guest appearances. I know that if anybody had suggested adding any of the above to my kit list in previous years I'd have just shrugged, no doubt with a bewildered look on my face; yet these are the times we're now living in, and if that means being just that bit safer, I'm happy to accept this in order to continue with my adventures.

As June wore on, I felt happy that I'd researched and then revised my kit list ahead of the lockdown ending: this was another important step in being ready to get out and about in nature more. There's such joy to be found in truly getting away from the constant buzz of towns and cities, and I decided that now was the time to rediscover that joy again.

So, at weekends, I'd get up early and head out, traipsing through local farm fields on the edge of town for a few hours. Whenever I looked back, I could see Maidenhead on the horizon, but instead of feeling like I couldn't completely shake off my urban location, I revelled in the fact that there was all this unexplored countryside so close to home.

Lockdown One (Mid-June to July) – Getting Back Out There

By 15th June shops were opening back up, but the way I'd decided to visit town had changed, at least for now: I'd go to town as infrequently as possible and very early in the day, having pre-planned the shops I needed to go to. These guerrilla-style tactics were required to get the job done as soon as possible. It was also time efficient, leaving me more time to plan or execute local adventures!

Finally, at the end of June, Robin and I met up in Maidenhead for a long overdue hike. We'd both packed our cooking gear and some grub and, after strolling beyond the farm fields that I'd re-energised myself in a few weeks before, we now espied the front line of the Chiltern Hills as we entered what we thought to be a secluded woodland. With grey clouds threatening rain, it was a good time to take cover under the foliage, and we soon identified a spot amongst a cluster of trees that we felt presented us with a good opportunity to cook without being disturbed.

After months of being hemmed in, this experience had a truly liberating effect on me: as the burgers sizzled on the portable stove, I realised I had intertwining butterflies of excitement and nervousness in my stomach. Or maybe that was my tummy rumbling – I'm not sure. Anyway, we demolished our feast, satisfied with adding this new element to our hiking.

As we'd eaten we'd occasionally heard voices around us, and we kept reassuring ourselves that we were so hidden we wouldn't be spotted. However, as we made a well-deserved brew, a couple waved at us from the path above where we were sitting. I grimaced as Robin calmly waved back.

'So much for stealth,' I said.

'If in doubt, act confident,' Robin answered. 'Most people are just curious.'

'Cheers,' I beamed, holding my cup aloft.

'Yeah, confident like that,' he chuckled.

Soon after, we packed up and made our way back. As we marched along a track adjacent to a farm field we were treated to the sight of a deer bolting through a hedge; we stopped in amazement, appreciating how this moment had made this hike so much more memorable. I'd heard of deer being out this way, but to see them so close really made me appreciate, yet again, what the local area had to offer.

Then, on 4th July, the first lockdown ended. There was no victory parade in the city streets, honking of car horns in celebration, or climbing monuments and waving flags; after all, we were still being constantly warned that the fight against the virus wasn't over.

Over the coming weeks, news reports showed people either swarming to venues like beaches and parks, or continuing to shield. I fell somewhere in the middle of the spectrum, picking my times to go out – usually early in the morning or late at night – to keep up my walks.

It was during this time that I started sitting in front of a small fire in my garden, discovering that it reduced any Covid-related anxiety due to its purifying and meditative nature. I'd focus my mind, visualising myself being out on hills far away from the throngs, actively going through all the phases of a journey – packing my bag, putting on my shoes, heading out on a train, alighting at a random village, and heading off into the woods – and I believe that such mindfulness gifted me with more encouragement to go off and explore when I could.

This first lockdown had been a complex and testing ordeal for all of us, in so many different and far-reaching ways.

Now, as summer kicked in, it was time to have some proper adventures – all, of course, while staying safe.

Handy tips

For Virtual Walks

Whilst it would be laborious to list every country and video suggestion for each, here I offer a few ideas to get you started on your world tour. In the YouTube search bar, type in the phrase 'Virtual Hike/Walk' followed by a country name, and see where it takes you. If you're interested in finding out more about certain countries, then do a bit of research to see which monuments, museums and parks there are in that particular country and look to see if there are any tours of those. To get you started, try searching 'British Museum Virtual Tour' or 'Vatican Virtual Tour'.

It's fair to say that some countries are better represented than others when it comes to virtual tours and hikes. if you find this to be the case, then try watching a documentary about a country on YouTube instead. For some countries you might find official tourist videos as well. Alternatively, you'll more than likely find a YouTuber who's put up a video of their visit to your chosen country (it's fair to say that some of these videos may not be of the best quality, though, and really quite short). The best YouTubers for doing a world tour from home include Drew Binsky and Gabriel Traveler.

Virtual Cycling

Similar advice applies to searching for cycling tours on YouTube: just pop in 'Virtual Cycling Tour' and the country of your choice into the search bar. At the time of writing, I'm not sure if all countries are represented. I just searched for 'Cycling Tour Of The World' and it seems that there are a plethora of YouTubers documenting their travels for you to cycle along with. Also, even though I don't own a motorbike, there's a community of YouTubers that have documented their travels on their bikes. For this, I can recommend the Itchy Boots channel to cycle along to in order to get you started.

Cooking

If you're interested in cooking outside, I'd recommend you start with a camping gas stove set-up. I've included some info in the Appendix on a cheap basic set-up to help get you started. Building fires is a particular skill and should only be attempted by an experienced hand in a safe environment, away from others. Two YouTubers who do outdoor fireside cooking and who I like watching are Kent Survival and Simon, A Bloke In The Woods.

Staying Safe When Out And About

The BMC's useful poster for advice on staying safe outside can be found at: https://www.thebmc.co.uk/bmc-launches-covid19-recovery-plan-for-climbing--hill-walking

The TGO magazine article reminding you to be mindful of touching gates, stiles and other manmade obstacles in the countryside can be found at: https://www.tgomagazine.co.uk/news/a-hill-walkers-guide-to-the-coronavirus-outbreak/

However, please note that, as advice may change over time, it's always best to follow the Government's advice at www.gov.uk

Chapter Fourteen

2020 PART 2

First Walks Of Summer

Situated in the countryside to the north-east of my hometown lies the Maidenhead Commons. In the early 1800s this was the site for The Brick and Tile Works that provided employment and housing for workers and their families in the local area. The brickworks shut down in 1968 and has since been home to much varied plant and pond life in its current guise as a nature reserve.

Robin and I had passed this spot a few weeks before when we'd had our first breakfast in the woods – only we'd not spotted it at the time! It was now two weeks after Lockdown One had ended and I was on an aimless wander in the same area on a clear blue sky day. Having noticed the reserve this time, my curiosity guided my path.

As I followed the set track, I revelled in the twin facts that not only had I found another new local scenic place to visit, but that I could also learn more about the history of the town where I lived.

I ambled between the information boards, taking in the wildlife of my surroundings: insects skittered on ponds filled with white lilies, and trees stood strong as if they'd been there for many an age (at first glance, I think I'd have been forgiven if I hadn't known this area had previously been a brickworks).

This site is now a National Trust protected area, so I knew I wouldn't be knocking up a cooked meal that day. However, I did see it as an opportunity to boost my stealth skills in order to help me gain confidence when we sought out future locations to conjure up some tasty grub. Normally, in such situations I'm about as surreptitious as somebody trying to get through airport customs in a suit of armour. Today, though, I was intent on performing amicably to achieve a higher level of culinary covertness.

Having completed a lap of the reserve, I'd shortlisted my target sites down to three locations. On further inspection, the first two didn't provide me with the cover I needed due to the fact that they were about 10 feet from the main path. The third one, however, was just right: I'd seen a gap amongst the trees that sloped down to a secluded area away from the path. Sheltered by the trees, I realised I should be able to trek further in. So, I took out my phone and consulted the map, acknowledging that I may indeed be able to go deeper.

At this stage I became a bit more casual, as I was sure I was well away from any prying eyes.

The next thing I knew, I was sitting on a tree stump protected by natural camouflage. As I listened to the birds chattering in the branches above and some dogs barking somewhere in the distance, I gave my stomach a pat on the back (as it were) in the best way I knew how: I ate some malt loaf.

As I munched away I contemplated how this year had taken so much from us, and yet we'd persevered, adapted, and carved out new stories of our own. All at once, I felt it was more possible for me to scrutinise my local area for new places of adventure and quiet contemplation – something that was both small and big in helping me cope with the changes we were all having to face, individually and collectively.

After about three-quarters of an hour, I packed up and spun around to take in my new local hideaway. I knew that, if needed, I now had a place I could visit to restore myself from time to time. Or, if national supplies for malt loaf were running low, I could escape here to hide my secret stash!

I'd gone out with the intention of exploring the outskirts of Maidenhead a little more, and now I was basking in how carefree I could be with hardly another soul in sight – a feeling that, woefully, I'd unintentionally lost during this addled year.

I followed country lanes, meandered through fields, and ended up in a local wood close to a pub. It's funny how you can pass a place so many times without any real intent; I'd been on this road so many times in previous years, but standing where I was now, under the lush green trees (and feeling grateful for the cooling respite from the sun), it seemed as if I was witnessing it for the first time.

Reluctantly, I pulled out my phone – I'd been trying to do this walk with the intention of free exploration – as the eagerness to find out where I was overwhelmed me.

I found myself in Goulding's Wood, a stretch of woods that form part of the Bisham Woods.

Kenneth Grahame strolled here when he lived in nearby Cookham, and the setting is said to have been a major influence on his book, *Wind In The Willows*. I didn't see Ratty, Mr Toad, Mole, or Badger this day, though; I only had the birds for company again.

Feeling inspired after uncovering this jewel of local history, I decided to go off the main track and explore further, heading into deeper woodland. The air was still and silent; I'd seen nobody since I'd entered.

The elation I experienced when I looked up and observed the sunlight flickering through the gaps in the leaves boosted me exponentially. This day was fast becoming the standout day of the year, given all that had come before. It dawned on me that, on most of my expeditions, I'd ventured far from home to get my kicks and to embrace the peace and quiet; now, I was revelling in the fact that I could do this so close to home.

'It's quite good here,' said a small voice.

'It is. It's been quite the adventure,' I replied.

'Can I go and climb that tree?' he asked.

'Okay, but be careful.'

My inner child legged it over to a line of trees as I watched on with a smile. My imagination was in full flow. Fallen tree trunks took on the form of mythical beasts as if frozen in battle: a fearsome dragon with gaping jaws here, a mega python waiting to strike there. This truly was an inspiring place, and in my heart I renamed it Dragonwood!

I had time to explore the rest of the Bisham Woods, but – despite the protestations of my inner child – it seemed appropriate to save any further surprises it could throw at me for another day. No wonder this area had inspired Kenneth Grahame – it was so worth visit after visit.

Indeed, a couple of weeks later I was back there with Robin, having enthused to him about the area.

After footslogging it through Goulding's Wood and crossing over a small country lane, we were now in Inkydown Wood. This stretch became more hilly, and it dawned on us that this could be an ideal training area for mountains. Further research showed that this area of ancient woodland had also been instrumental in providing building material for Windsor Castle, although we found no signs of a quarry. After navigating some steeper footpaths, we approached the end of the woods and noted an ice store that used to supply ice for Bisham Abbey.

It was a sultry day and soon we were bolting past the Bisham Abbey Sports Centre. Had we not been so thirsty, we'd have slowed down to take in the significance of where we were. However, in the near distance we'd become aware of a place of far more significance in that moment: a pub!

I'd been putting off visits to ale houses since the first lockdown had lifted. Now, though, the need for rehydration had gone beyond a level that mere water could quench.

As we stepped in, I was relieved to see that social distancing measures were being adhered to. Furthermore, being quite cautious by nature, I was surprised at how easily I settled into being back in a pub. The past few months had bombarded our brains, changing the way we viewed activities and places. Taking all the necessary Covid-19 precautions was essential – but we both benefited mentally from doing something that was so normal.

After this, we wound our way back into the wood via a Norman church. Here, the graveyard sloped naturally into the Thames, while sun-kissed farm fields stretched into the distance beyond the opposite bank.

'We need to explore these woods more often,' Robin said once we were back in Inkydown Wood.

'I reckon this place is worthy of a visit in every season,' I replied.

'Plus, now we can begin going a little further afield,' Robin offered.

'Definitely,' I concurred. 'It's good to know we've got more on offer close to home as well.'

Kayak Attack

Over the next few weeks, we decided that Berkshire was going to be our playground. In early August, we hiked near to Robin's house in another wood that was also worthy of future exploration. As we'd done on the Bisham Woods walk, we sought out places that could provide us with cover to do a secret cooking experiment. We hadn't given up on this idea; we were just caught up in the moment of finding new places to explore. Again, that sense of freedom I'd experienced on my first trek to Goulding's Wood kicked in, and it was so easy to get lost in the thought of being a 10-year-old Tarzan again.

Although we hadn't experienced any mountains and barely any hills, the spirit for new adventures had certainly gripped us. Then, in early September, Robin suggested going kayaking.

Do you remember how I instantly ruled myself out of going up Snowdon after the ordeal that was Scafell Pike? Well, I think that by replying 'yes' straight away to going out on the water showed that the days of being Mr Mega Cautious were well behind me. I didn't give the fact that I can't swim a second thought.

I'd never tried kayaking before so, when the day came, I felt very excited. As I travelled there on an empty train – a surreal experience for a Saturday between Maidenhead and Reading – I was looking forward to my inner child being in full flow again.

As the train rolled out of my hometown, I recalled when Robin had put forward the point that if we became decent enough at kayaking, a new world of possibilities would open up as to what we could do outdoors. Upon hearing this, thoughts of a hiking-kayaking-camping adventure had illuminated my mind like neon lights. I'd been exercising fairly well over the past few months, and so I believed I was in good enough shape to take on this new challenge.

I met Robin at the kayaking centre, and as we paddled out from the shore I smiled like a whacky kid grinning inanely into the camera on school photo day. There was hardly a soul about; if my inexperience showed through, it wouldn't matter too much.

The serene lake was slate grey, reflecting the sky, and at its centre was an island. We agreed to aim for this island, circumnavigate around it, and then head back to the shore. I'd watched a few YouTube videos instructing me on how to use a paddle correctly, and it pleased me when – after about five minutes – I realised I'd been keeping a straight line and only veering left or right when needed.

As my movements became almost automatic, I began to daydream of weekends paddling up rivers and trekking hills. My attention was brought back to the present moment, however, as my lower back began to spasm; my body seized and I couldn't unlock my muscles or joints.

'Are you okay?' asked a concerned Robin.

'My back is giving me gyp,' I said as I lay down in my kayak.

'We'll be at the island soon. Try and pull through, then we'll assess it from there,' he said reassuringly.

'Okay, you go on and I'll catch you up.'

I lay there for a few moments, looking up at the clouds, trying to focus on the movement of the vessel rocking gently on the water as I breathed deeply in and out. Soon the pain had passed and I was able to sit up again. Tentatively, I rotated my arms as I rolled gently across the surface to catch up with Robin. However, within seconds I was lying on my back again as electric pain struck my spine.

This time, the throbbing ache intensified all over my back and I became concerned about rolling over into the drink. Despite the fact that I was wearing a life jacket, I became more rigid as I recalled that I couldn't swim.

As the pain subsided once more, I poked my head up like a petrified cartoon mouse attempting to come out from its hiding place.

I rolled my shoulders and adjusted myself into my seat once more.

'Come on, mate. You can make it!' Robin hollered encouragingly.

'I'm gonna have to head back to shore,' I moaned. 'You carry on.'

Robin paused for a moment. 'I can head back with you if you want.'

'It's okay. I'll race you back.'

He smiled and accepted the challenge.

I spun my boat around and maintained a steady-ish line back to land, pausing twice as my back jolted again.

Back at the shoreline, as I attempted to step out of the boat, my legs went from beneath me and I fell back into the water as if I'd been knocked down by a heavyweight boxer. Thankfully, the water was shallow here and all I suffered was a wet backside and a bruised ego.

I scanned for a safe, people-free spot to wait for Robin on the sand.

'You'll be needing to do more arm exercises, then,' chuckled Robin after I recounted my story to him.

'I think it'll be a few days at least before I'll exercise again,' I answered.

'Still, don't be discouraged. It's only your first time.'

'True, and I was enjoying it until my back gave up on me.'

I knew there and then that I'd try more kayaking even though my first attempt had been a tragicomedy. The thrill of being able to go and explore the outdoors in new ways had soaked into my DNA.

When You're In A Rut, Go To Rutland

2020 had limited us, and the day-to-day monotony of living under a pandemic had made us crave variety. After going kayaking we had a renewed spirit for adventure, and we didn't want to stop.

There's so much joy to be found being out in the wilderness – becoming lost in the moment in the name of 'getting away from it all' – and now we were keen to experience it in yet more different ways. Getting out on a lake again would lift our souls (and quite possibly put my back out), but still we desired something else. Hiking and canoeing could easily be combined for deeper countryside experiences, but what could we add on to that?

'Cycling!' announced Aaron over a video chat one mid-September Saturday evening.

My stomach flipped immediately. I hadn't used a bike in about twenty-odd years – not counting my mini pedal exerciser – and whenever we'd been on a hike in recent times I'd always been wary and curious of cyclists. Wary because of how you can be enjoying a peaceful trek only for some Lycra-clad busybody to appear out of nowhere and zoom past you like a howitzer, leaving about an inch gap between you both; you being left with your arms flailing as you try to recentre yourself to avoid falling into a hedge. And curious because I just couldn't see how people could enjoy rural settings by buzzing around at top speed, missing what was right in front of them.

Fair enough, these thoughts apply to a minority rather than the polite majority, but having seen my fair share of dudes on two wheels whilst out and about, I thought my opinion had some grounding.

'Challenge your own perspective,' Robin said.

'How?' I asked, confused.

'Er...go cycling!' Aaron replied.

'Yeah, let's have a socially distanced break,' offered Robin.

'A cycling holiday?' I enquired.

There were nods and smiles all round.

'We've had to keep things small this year, so why don't we go to the smallest UK county?' asked Robin.

'Rutland!' Aaron and I cried out in unison.

My heart hammered so rapidly in my chest I thought it would smash through my ribcage. We were going away and... err...I'd be on a bike.

About three weeks later, on a drizzly Saturday mid-October afternoon, the tents were pitched and we were ready to go on a tri-county hike encompassing the borders of Northamptonshire, Leicestershire, and Rutland. The planning for all our previous adventure trips had involved diligent (if a bit laid back) planning; for this expedition, though, the strategising had to be ultra-military style: searching for a campsite that had spot-on social distancing guidelines was a high-level assignment in itself.

After much deliberation, Robin had found a farm campsite that we were all comfortable with.

As we headed out of the farm, I looked back and took in the extra space between the pitches, noting how we'd all become used to this surreal but now necessary way of living.

By the time we'd reached the pub for grub that evening, we'd surely broken our personal bests for walking across farm fields. Although our views were limited by rain and mist, it was clear that this tri-county area was stunning, with the greens, oranges and crimsons of autumn giving it a rich, earthy glow.

It was great catching up with Aaron again too as he enthused about our bike ride in the morning.

'Seventeen miles or so around Rutland Water,' he said as he supped his pint.

I stopped supping my own pint and stared at him, gobsmacked. 'I'm gobsmacked,' I said back.

'You'll be fine if you're keeping fit. Just think of it as hiking up a very long, very high mountain,' Robin answered philosophically.

About 10.30 a.m. the next morning, we commenced our mission from a car park close to the village of Egleton. Until we reached our first stop near the wonderful 'floating' church at Normanton, I'd been hurtling along with a facial expression akin to Popeye doing a parachute jump. Boats pootled about on the lake and day trippers traversed its shores. Here and there, anglers had pitched up, hoping to get a catch.

Riding at high speed through woodland trails and paths that straddled the water was exhilarating. There was a moderate number of people out this day and we were well able to keep our space as we went.

The second part of the course became more hilly, and at these points I'd jump off the bike and walk. At one point, my heart sank as a couple in their seventies whizzed past me on their bikes; only when Aaron told me they were on electric bikes did I feel relieved. Soon, though, we'd be on pavements next to busy stretches of motorway, and I could make up time before riding back in to the more forested areas. Even if the area was toned down in numbers of visitors thanks to the current climate, it was clear to see why this area remains a popular destination for anybody with a sense of adventure – or just anyone looking for a dose of fresh air and some pleasant views.

After we'd completed our giant lap, the honour fell to me as the last one back to grab our snacks from a café near the car park.

'I like it here,' exclaimed Robin as he slurped his ice cream.

'Yeah, it's buzzing,' smiled Aaron.

'Fishing, cycling, hiking, bird-watching, and watersports,' I said, looking at a leaflet on the area.

'We're coming back, aren't we?' nodded Aaron.

'Yeahhhh,' Robin and I concurred.

It was great to get away from it all and do something like this, and catching up with Aaron had been a blast. We'd had reservations about social distancing and the numbers of people who might be out and about, but it all worked out fine.

On the way back, I reflected on my previous views on cycling. I'd enjoyed the countryside in full at a higher speed than usual, and we'd managed to stay respectfully clear of other cyclists and hikers enjoying the day. I like it when my self-contained views are challenged and I can learn something from the experience, allowing me to grow as a person. Sure, I admit I'll still be wary of MAMILs (Middle-Aged Men In Lycra) burning past us on their bikes, but my perspective of the world on wheels has permanently changed.

A few days after, it became clear to me, yet again, how much hiking had given us. By starting out one day and simply putting one foot in front of the other, we were now grasping at new ways to explore the country.

Useful Links

For The Brick and Tile Works, Maidenhead – https://www.nationaltrust.org.uk/maidenhead-and-cookham-commons/features/brick-and-tile-works-at-maidenhead-commons

For Goulding's and Bisham Woods – https://www.woodlandtrust.org.uk/visiting-woods/woods/bisham-woods

For Rutland Water – www.anglianwaterparks.co.uk

Chapter Fifteen

2020 PART 3

A couple of weeks after the Rutland excursion, the UK went into another lockdown in another attempt to stop the virus spreading. It was time to adapt again and look into doing different activities to pass the time.

<u>Virtual Hikes Evolve</u>

I'd carried on with my virtual video hikes across different countries and continents throughout the year – albeit with a bit of a dip in the summer as we ventured out a bit more – and I'd been contemplating mixing it up for a while.

I started by experiencing as many different mountain ranges as possible. If I couldn't find a virtual hike up a mountain pass, then I'd walk along to a documentary of some climbers; again, I noticed how sweaty my palms would get even from the safety of my front room as I watched these mountaineering dudes climb over rock faces at 6,000+ metres. However, I was grateful for the chance to continue combatting my phobia of heights.

During the first week of the second lockdown, I went a-hiking in Yerevan, the capital of Armenia. It occurred to me then that I could potentially visit every capital city in the world. After popping the names of a few random capitals along with the phrase 'virtual walk' into the search engine, I enthused that this could be a sustainable hobby to keep me going through what could be a very long winter.

I thought about what I wanted to achieve, and soon I'd devised a format and a few rules: I'd stroll around three capitals per week minimum for at least thirty minutes; if I wasn't able to find a decent virtual hiking video of a certain capital, I'd watch a documentary-style video of that capital or country; then I'd write down each capital I'd visited along with how long I'd spent there and how many steps I took. I also decided to learn a little of the history and culture of each country along the way – sure, this wasn't the totally immersive experience of actually being in these wonderful destinations, but it certainly gave me a chance to appreciate the world in a new light.

At the time of writing (mid-January 2021) I've so far racked up over 50 countries, and there have been some amazing highlights: Dushanbe in Tajikistan was pleasantly peaceful, surrounded by breathtaking mountains; the streets of Buenos Aires I marched down were delightfully bohemian and sun-kissed; Andorra was the jewel of the Pyrenees, captivating me as if it were a long-lost kingdom with all the mod cons; and I really want to visit Barbados now. I've also seen places where's a lack of wealth and infrastructure – and, no doubt, I'll see plenty more of those – but the main lesson I'm taking away from these snapshots of my time in other countries is that life always carries on in some way, and people are generally warm and friendly.

Over time, I've discovered that the quality of the videos can vary, and sometimes I'm in the hands of a YouTuber who shoots off in some random direction that is far different than where they intended to go. However, I've generally been able to whittle my list of go-to channels down to about five or six, with some quality cameos along the way. If this is a challenge you'd like to take up, I've left a few suggestions in the handy tips section of this chapter and in the Appendix.

Overall, I'd say travelling the world by YouTube is worthwhile because, even if you are only in one place for a short time, you begin to amass whole new perspectives on different places you might otherwise never get to see. Of course, it's also a free way to travel the globe!

Adopting a Virtual Reality Mindset

Still craving mountains, it had stayed in the back of my mind throughout 2020 that the progress I'd made in working on my acrophobia could become redundant. Mountain videos and documentaries had certainly given me a lift and kept my mind primed to a degree, but something else was needed if I wanted to keep up my advancements.

I put this forward to Robert on the phone one November evening. He said that he'd discovered Virtual Reality games on his phone, telling me it's possible to buy a set of cardboard VR goggles at a very inexpensive price. He also typed 'Acrophobia VR' into the android store on his mobile and listed the names of a few apps I could try. I ordered a set of VR goggles right away and looked forward to starting off on this new little adventure.

A few days later, I'd completed my first session of VR mountain walking. It had been a heady trek across a mountainous island with peaks growing higher and higher as I patrolled this fantasy landscape. Dizzy and disorientated after only a few minutes, I convinced my bamboozled brain that it needed to become accustomed to this. 2020 had presented me with a severe lack of opportunities for being at altitude, and now, my determination to persevere and acclimatise outweighed any alternative behaviour. Although sweat slid off my palms and I experienced some bizarre giggling fits, the ecstasy of being in this moment filled me with joy. I...was...on...a...mountain!

My initial attempt ended after about 20 minutes, when I clattered into the clothes horse in the kitchen! A state of nausea washed over me and I had to have a sit-down with a strong, sweet mug of tea. Then I had another mug of tea, and decided to persevere with this endeavour each evening until I didn't get the sweats anymore.

In another app I was able to take a jetpack ride across a city and, initially, giddiness overwhelmed me. However, soon enough I'd adapted and was enjoying the thrill of flying above all the buildings.

Since the end of the second lockdown, I've played these games two or three times a week. There are many more games available for high altitude lovers – rollercoaster VR is quite enthralling – but these are the two games I enjoy the most. I'm hopeful that doing this has boosted my confidence for when we're back on one of our epic journeys again.

Walking Meditation

As I've repeatedly tried to demonstrate in this book, walking is an excellent way of switching off from the world and reclaiming yourself. Just give me a hill, a pork pie, a sunny day, and the music of Kurt Cobain – now that's instant Nirvana! (Grunge rock may not be your thing, but listening to your favourite music on a stroll can enhance your mood wherever you are.) It was whilst thinking about all this at home one day – though I was listening to Idlewild and not Nirvana at the time – that I had a realisation that caused me to have brain sparks: walking is a form of meditation.

After a quick Google search, I found a BUPA podcast on walking mindfulness. In a basic sense, the practice teaches you to engage each of your senses in turn in order to focus on all you can see, hear, touch, and smell as you amble or march along. Plus, it's also good to take note of how your body moves. The practice can be performed anywhere: at home, in the shops, walking in the countryside, strolling in Luton...just use your imagination. This way of exercising is also said to boost well-being and to improve attention skills as it keeps your mind in the here and now, thus increasing your appreciation of your surroundings.

After listening to a few walking meditations on YouTube, I soon had several techniques logged into my noggin. It was fun trying this out on various rambles in the woods or through the streets; I enjoyed how sounds and colours became more intense. Engrossing the mind in such a way has proven effective time and time again in terms of having a good old mental declutter.

Please see the handy tips section below for a few ideas to get you started. You may find that, after listening to a few walking meditations, you discover other techniques too.

Cooking Under A Canopy

This second lockdown wasn't as strict as the first, and it was still possible to meet one other person in an outdoor setting. In one sense it didn't limit me and Robin, as we could still navigate local areas in the name of adventure; however, we needed to do so with responsibility and vigilance. With November kicking in as well, the days were shorter and so our explorations needed to be squeezed into a smaller number of hours.

Usually, at this time of year, the distances we could have walked in a day would also be limited if we stopped off at a pub for lunch. Now, we could have taken a packed lunch, but we didn't want to miss a warming meal on a dreary day – the prospect of which can be so uplifting when it comes from getting from A to B. In cooking alfresco, our local odysseys had given us more confidence – and the knowhow we needed to secure quiet locations where we could cook.

During November and December, we became quite efficient at executing our plans. The slapdash, on-the-fly approach – which is my default style most of the time – was replaced by forthright planning, so that as soon as we were pitched up in the woods we were frying up burgers, sausages and eggs, and brewing up tea. The tricky transportation of liquids such as cooking oil and milk were overcome by replacing them with substitutes like spray-based frying oil and milk powder. Issues such as avoiding kneeling down in wet mud were controlled by having an inexpensive durable plastic sheet to rest upon. We enjoyed, then, how the whole experience encouraged us to be more creative with our solutions.

During one of our escapades, Robin remarked that to be in nature with a freshly made hot drink – instead of one from a flask – was really rewarding. And, of course, there's also the buzz of completely slowing down and appreciating your surroundings with satisfied bellies!

Layers have definitely been added to our hiking experiences, and when we talk about the skills, wisdom, and escapades that nature has given us, we feel truly blessed.

Although our meals have only been basic fry-ups up to this point, it's surely only a matter of time before we expand on what we're making – and another adventure lies therein.

Handy tips

Hiking The World's Capitals

To reiterate, put the name of a capital city into the YouTube search engine along with a phrase such as 'walking tour' or 'virtual tour'. The video tours for some capitals may not be of a decent length and the quality of the production may vary; to counter this, perhaps watch a combination of documentaries, tourism company videos, and short walking videos on that capital/country to make up the desired time you'd like to walk for. Feel free to use the guidelines I mentioned above or set some rules of your own.

To get you started, a couple of channels I often use are POP-travel and Expedia Travel. You might also come to know various globetrotting YouTubers you can fall back on; one of my favourites is Gabriel Traveler.

Virtual Reality

An inexpensive pair of cardboard VR goggles to use with your smartphone can be found at: https://www.amazon.co.uk/Virtual-Real-Store-Comfortable-Smartphones/dp/B072ZYWVS5

The VR fantasy mountain island I play is 'VR Relaxation Walking in Virtual Reality 2' by Pawel Patrzek.

The jetpack game is a section in the app 'Walk The Plank VR' by Applications-B.

(Both games are available in the Google Play Store.)

Walking Meditation

BUPA Podcast: https://www.bupa.co.uk/newsroom/ourviews/mindful-walking-meditation#:~:text=Mindful%20walking%20is%20a%20form,focus%20on%20the%20present%20moment.

A couple of ideas for YouTube videos:

https://youtu.be/xXYFNmFb6zY (from The Mindful Movement Channel)

https://youtu.be/8D3oh2Rdvyw (from the Great Meditation Channel)

Or, just type the phrase 'walking meditation' into the YouTube search engine and take your pick of what's on offer.

Section Three:

ADVICE AND GUIDANCE

Chapter Sixteen

WHY I WALK

The biggest advantage I've found with walking is that it allows me to completely de-stress from life. Whether I'm happy or sad, a good dose of country air and some spectacular views of rolling green fields cause joyous rapture in my heart and bring about a positive state of mind. When I'm out in the open I become detached from the rigours of life, and because of this I'm able to tackle them afresh; time slows down and whatever challenges I'm facing in that current moment seem to become less significant. As a result, my sense of self-worth immediately increases. It is, quite simply, magic.

Plus, there's the adventure side as well.

Sure, going on a day hike along rivers, through fields, and up hills doesn't sound as grand as doing a globe-trekking multi-adventure, yet after a decent ramble I come back feeling enriched with a pocketful of stories to tell about the places I've seen, the people I've met, and/or the incidents that have occurred. Most importantly, all of this inspires me to write. The two activities just seem so intertwined to me, as it allows the memories I have of my wonderful, perspective-changing walks to become permanent. Plus, in a way, I'm tracking my progress and development as I gain more experience – even if I'm prone to being rather hapless from time to time (though I would argue that my haplessness adds more flavour to my escapades).

All this calls out to my soul. When I'm perched atop a hill on a sunny day, I wish that moment could last for eternity, especially when the serenity of such moments is aided by the gentle sounds of nature. This ultimate peace has become so alive within me since I began walking as a hobby, and I truly believe it is something that's made me a more optimistic person overall.

Undertaking a solo trek helps me learn more about myself and assists me with developing new mindsets. I'm definitely more patient nowadays – even the thought of knowing I'll be going on a walk in a few days' time has a calming effect on me (most of the time) – and becoming a hill fanatic has largely contributed to that.

Exploring the Great Green Beyond is an obvious way to escape your day-to-day routine and the inevitable information overload we all have to deal with on a daily basis.

However, statistics can be important in walking, as long as this doesn't mean that all the natural beauty on offer is sacrificed. Numbers are essential when creating a sense of achievement: how many miles I've walked, how many steps I've taken, how many calories I've burned. Is it possible to squeeze in an extra few miles today? Doing a 10-mile walk, hitting 20,000 steps, or pushing myself to go that little bit further is such a rewarding experience each and every time. I've been out there, done something, gone further than I ever have before, and enjoyed it even more.

I'm always conscious to combine that sense of personal achievement with taking in the splendour of the hills, forests, and river towpaths I stride. It's a double celebration.

I've also learnt new skills with regards to planning my own routes, or following – sometimes questionable – walking guides from the internet. And then there's the freedom that comes in not planning at all; just waiting for Saturday to roll around so I can jump on a train and be spontaneous, heading in whichever direction I choose in the moment. As I've shown, however, having a sense of direction like mine – which often results in becoming lost or encountering some other obstacle – can be an issue; yet, I think such hindrances can only add to the memory of an adventure!

As well as the mental and soul benefits to walking, there are many physical health-based advantages too, including a healthier heart, weight loss, and stronger muscles and bones. Walking also helps combat the effects of depression and anxiety, as well as lowering the risk of such conditions as stroke, diabetes, and arthritis. Remember at the start of this book when I said I used to be rooted to the sofa, watching hours and hours of TV whilst eating a wide range of snacks? Well, I can definitely say that walking has helped me become less fatigued – though, admittedly, I still struggle rather a lot with the snacking part!

In this book I've focused on the joy of going on walks either alone or with friends, in the hopes of inspiring readers to make those small changes themselves and to go and enjoy The Outside. There's also the wider social aspect when it comes to walking, with different rambling groups offering options for people of varying abilities. Back in 2017, I did a quick Google search for local walking groups and noticed groups for the elderly, disabled persons, and pregnant women (there are groups for people of all backgrounds – just try searching for a local hiking group that suits your circumstances, or even create one yourself through a social activities website such as www.meetup.com).

Robin had previously discovered Meetup, finding a number of hiking groups within a few miles of where we lived. The set-up suited us as it meant we could join these groups for one-off walks here and there without any long-term, continuous commitment. There was a small fee to pay per event, but the beauty of these walks was that somebody else organised them, freeing us up to relax and enjoy all the trek had to offer.

During one group walk we did in the Chilterns back in 2017, the group leader explained to us that there was generally a rotating core that would do such hikes, then there would be other regulars who came and went, and then there were those who were just in the area for the weekend, looking for something fun and energetic to do. Of course, meeting people from all different backgrounds is really good for building social skills, too.

As time went on, we became increasingly confident in striking out on our own, enjoying having the countryside to ourselves.

Having a more personal relationship with the countryside became deeply rewarding. Organised groups certainly have their place, though, and I'd say they certainly have their merits for anybody who's just starting out – they can see if hiking is right for them, and consider whether they'd like to mix with a wider group of people.

Another great thing about walking is that it can be done cheaply; all you need to start are the clothes you wear and a pair of trainers and you're off – just take a snack and a drink from home too.

Even though nothing beats the countryside, towns are still worthy of exploration; it really is amazing what you can learn about your own area simply by putting one foot in front of the other and actually paying attention to your surroundings. Doing the same journey at different times of the day – or at different times of the year – can be stimulating too.

Walking feeds the mind, body, and soul.

Plus, there's the other big advantage: placing one foot in front of the other will also, eventually, lead me to a pub.

Chapter Seventeen

KIT LIST AND STAYING SAFE

What you take with you on a hike – and when – will depend on several factors such as the weather, the altitude, the duration of your walk, and how remote of an area you'll be trekking in. Therefore, it's best to check websites that offer advice on what to take on day hikes (this can be done by putting words such as 'day hiking kit list' into Google) and for the particular journey (mountain or otherwise) you're taking e.g. 'Ben Nevis day hiking kit list'.

When on a hike, your biggest priority should always be safety, and being prepared is key. As a rule, the longer you're outside, the more food, water, and clothing you may need. Personally, I'm still learning a lot, but thanks to my research I've invested in some important pieces of equipment (see below) should the need arise.

Here then – as a means to get you started – is my list of essential items I take on hikes. This list is not definitive and it's certainly not exhaustive; I still add to mine every now and then. Please also note, this is only a guide to the kinds of equipment and kit you'll need. As such, I won't be offering the names of product brands here as I genuinely feel there's true joy to discovering a convenient bit of kit for yourself.

Rucksack

The type and size of rucksack you require depends on the length and kind of hike you're going to do. I have a cheap fold-up one I use for urban walks and that's useful for storing my wallet, phone, keys, and any food and drink I want to take. I then have a larger, sturdier backpack for countryside hikes and hillwalking.

Food

Sandwiches, pasties, protein bars, crisps, and fruit are main staples for our hikes. Even if you know there's going to be a pub lunch stop along the way, taking a protein bar or two is always a good idea – just in case. From the Aston walk (Chapter 10) I learnt that food – even if you're only taking a small amount with you – should never be overlooked.

Water

The amount needed varies from person to person, and the distance, the weather, and the length of your walk are all factors that will affect this. Body weight and sweat rate have an impact too, but the more you walk, the more you'll have an idea of how much you'll need to drink on any given hike. As a starting point, for longer hikes I'd suggest taking four half-litre bottles of water and seeing how you go from there. Whilst breaking out into the open country has tempting perks, if you're just starting out then making sure there's a shop or pub nearby to stock up on water is no bad thing.

Fully charged mobile and spare battery

Mobile phones have so many functions – camera, internet for research, maps, note-taking apps – that can really enhance a walk. Of course, having a fully charged phone is important in case you need to call the emergency services while you're out in the countryside.

Map and compass

Basic map-reading and compass skills can't be substituted, especially when your phone is out of range and you can't rely on GPS. At the time of writing, I'm still learning how to use a compass; I've learnt that the majority of maps are oriented with north at the top, and that by finding magnetic north on my compass I've increased my chances of finding my bearings and not getting lost – which is easier said than done with me!

Torch

While most of us have torches on our phones nowadays, it's always useful to take a separate, battery-powered torch should your phone run out of juice – or in case you want to save your phone battery to look at maps and/or make emergency calls if needed.

Notepad and pen

These are handy to record memories – or to draw landscapes, if you're into that kind of thing. Paper can also be used as kindling if you're lost and need to start an emergency fire.

Spare change

This may come in handy if your phone fails you and you need to make an emergency call – as long as there's a phone box nearby.

First aid kit

This is self-explanatory, and you don't have to carry a massive one – a miniature first aid kit will help you in many situations too.

Midge repellent

Always handy, but especially if you're going hiking in certain places and at certain times of the year.

Paracord or string

This may come in handy if you get lost and need to make an emergency shelter. The one I have comes complete with a compass, whistle, and firestarter, so it's extra useful.

Bin bag

You can use this as an extra layer to stay dry, and it can also act as a cover for a makeshift shelter. I recently read a story about a guy who kept a large durable one with him at all times, just in case he ever got caught in the wilderness overnight and needed to use it as a sleeping bag.

Portable water filter device

There are many types of these devices on the market, and I've recently bought one that is in the shape of a straw. By removing all sorts of nasty bacteria and viruses from the water, it allows the user to drink from streams or rivers when they're without bottled water. The hope is that, if I sweat profusely through fear the next time I'm up a mountain and consequently end up draining my bottled water supply, I can still access a nearby stream.

Emergency sleeping bag and tent

These are extra-large, light tin foil sheets that pack away compactly, and the best part is, both of mine came in at under a tenner. These are items I haven't had to use yet, but I'm so glad they're there if I need them.

Portable multi-tool

I'll be honest – mine mainly gets used for cutting pork pies. Or that time when there was a fat caterpillar on the towpath and we were worried about it being trampled on. Robin suggested I let it crawl onto the device – which had previously been used to halve a pork pie – so that it could be moved and dispatched safely under an adjacent hedge. Still, this is an essential bit of kit if ever there was one.

Walking/trekking poles

These provide extra security if you're worried about walking on rough terrain or up sleep stopes where you think you might slip or stumble.

Since becoming a convert to the benefits of the great outdoors, it's nice to think that I've learnt several new skills and that I'm becoming better with the equipment I own – even if my application of the skills required is sometimes rather suspect. Hiking has taught me so much – and given me so much – which is why getting out and about in the countryside continues to excite me.

Clothing

Woolly hat
Moisture-reducing t-shirt
Fleece/jumper
Waterproof jacket
Hiking trousers
Waterproof trousers
Waterproof socks
Sturdy hiking boots
Bin bag (extra waterproof layer)
Gloves
Sunglasses
Scarf/Snood

Costs

In terms of the costs of the items mentioned above, the best advice is to shop around. You needn't buy the most expensive items out there; they just need to carry out their function(s) well. Before you commit to buying, read reviews on shopping websites or on walking blogs by people who have tested the gear themselves; YouTube videos are also useful ways of getting ideas for hiking essentials. You can always go into specialist outdoor shops and ask the staff for advice on building up a kit.

Looking at all of the above, it may seem like this is an expensive hobby. However, obtaining hiking-based items is something I've done over time in order to keep costs down. I've only ever bought products that are well within my budget and have sometimes asked for items as birthday or Christmas presents.

I'll total the cost of my default hiking kit here to give you an idea (though other items would be added depending on the length and severity of the hike):

Clothes: Hiking boots (£35); waterproof trousers (£20); sweat-reducing t-shirt (£3); fleece jumper (£3); waterproof jacket (£20); woolly hat (£3); gloves (£5); snood (£1).

Gear: Rucksack (£10); torch (£5); first aid kit (£7).

That's a total of £112, but remember: each item is durable and won't need to be replaced for a while.

Websites like Amazon and eBay offer you the chance to purchase the things you need for a reasonable price. Specialist hiking and outdoor stores can also offer a lot of products at reasonable prices. Just to reiterate: spending time researching the reliability of the product or item is an important step, because what you pay for needs to function well in all types of terrain and weather.

In short, do your research and stay within budget.

(Again, if money is tight, remember that going for a hike can be as simple as leaving your front door and exploring your own town and the local countryside for a few hours, without having to splash out on any new gear. Just remember to be sensible and stay safe.)

One final word: for any new product you buy, please read the manufacturer's instructions first. They're there for a reason.

Staying safe when out and about

Before you venture out and about in the English and Welsh countryside, the Country Access Code (www.gov.uk/government/publications/the-countryside-code) is worth looking at. Not only does it inform you of your rights of way, but it also tells you how to show consideration for all around you. Ordnance Survey Explorer and Landranger maps show most public rights of way.

For Scotland, the Scottish Outdoor Access Code can be found at www.outdooraccess-scotland.scot.

You should also be prepared for bad weather in any situation (especially at higher levels, where the weather can deteriorate rapidly).

I hope that by reading some of the walks I've described in this book, you can see the importance of having enough layers: whether on lowland or highland walks, warm and waterproof clothing is essential.

As I mentioned above, having enough food and water, a first aid kit, torch, whistle, map, compass, spare change, and a mobile phone are also incredibly important. Treading the paths of those who have put walks up on the internet is fun – especially as somebody else has already done the planning for you – but please be wary that these walks may be out of date; in such cases, it's worth checking your own maps (including Google Maps on your phone) ahead of the walk so you have an idea of the location of the nearest village, town, or city.

Before heading out, check the weather forecast for the area you're visiting and plan accordingly for the walk.

Always let somebody know where you're going and, ideally, finish walks well before nightfall.

There's no shame in having to abandon a route or change direction.

And (though hopefully I don't have to tell you this), take your litter with you.

If – like me with my fear of heights – you have something that holds you back and you really don't want to carry on, then don't. You've tried it, it's not worked out – and that's okay. Just pick a new place and a new route for next time. Don't be reckless!

Solo hikes can be great fun, but walking with at least one other person can be great as well, especially if you ever find yourselves in any kind of danger – in which case, having someone else with you is invaluable. (Also, there were definitely times on mountain walks when I wanted to completely give up right there and then, but with the support of my friends I was able to continue, ending up achieving some wonderful feats.)

If you're just beginning hiking and would like to explore hills and mountains, make sure you start out small. There's no point undertaking a massive trek only to find that – halfway up a mountain – it's not for you, or worse, that you're petrified out of your wits to the point where you may become a danger to yourself and others.

Start small; do walks in lowland countryside then build them up, taking on a few hills and going from there. You'll learn things about yourself in these situations that will benefit you greatly when you take on higher peaks – and that experience could be invaluable. Or, you may find that hill and mountain walking isn't your thing and that's that. Either way, you've taken the steps to start safely.

It's also worth visiting the Mountain Rescue website at www.mountain.rescue.org.uk/mountain-advice for some good info on how to stay safe.

As this book is mainly about day hikes, I won't go into things like making fires or building emergency shelters – you can find out about all that kind of stuff online if you need to. Having only ever done day hikes, I haven't had to do this myself, and if you're just starting out I only recommend doing day hikes anyway.

Finally, and importantly, the Coronavirus Pandemic has meant that additional items have had to be added to all kit lists – please see the FIRST 2020 CHAPTER (page 121).

Chapter Eighteen

DEALING WITH HEIGHTS

If I'd given my fear of heights considerable thought back in 2016, I think I'd have opted out of taking on Scafell Pike. Ignorance became a key factor, then, in me making it to Cumbria to tackle England's highest point. I clearly remember how I was on that hike: sweating copiously, fear encompassing me on the ascent as the valley floor below grew further and further away, and then – on the way down – trying to negotiate steep rocky pathways as my tired legs locked, almost feeling like they were about to snap.

After talking myself into going up Snowdon, I committed to taking on hills as a kind of exposure therapy in order to build myself up, preparing me for trekking up to the roof of Wales. This really helped me – plus, by then I was a lot fitter than I had been the previous summer.

Developing endurance and fitness became an essential part of my preparation for going up Ben Nevis too: the less physically tired I was, the more I could focus on negotiating the terrain rather than finding the whole task a complete slog. Even at the toughest points, I'd check myself, making sure I was physically okay to carry on – though it was clear at such points that it was more of a mental battle for me than physical.

One thing Snowdon offered that Scafell Pike didn't was wider paths that acted as a buffer zone to the slopes, making the Welsh route far more preferable to me. The fear and panic that comes from being on a narrow pathway can only be conquered by an incessant need to simply get the walk done, even if every footstep has to be slowly analysed as a whole throng of people pass me by. Ben Nevis had clearly defined paths but the sheer drop, I believe, is what really got to me.

It seems that narrow, rocky pathways and/or sheer drops are what give me the most cause for concern.

So why put myself through it if it's so mentally taxing and I end up being scared senseless? Well, I love hiking. I love high up places. I love the solitude. I love being able to conquer my fears. I do, however, need to be cautious, and my friends understand that if I think a climb is becoming too much, I'll have no qualms in turning back. Also, I'd have no trouble in ruling myself out of a climb if I felt it was too risky to begin with.

I've learnt that being prepared is key, and I now know the importance of taking more than enough water and food in order to stay hydrated and keep my energy levels up. Walking poles are an essential item that help provide an extra level of security, and wearing the right kind of clothing (e.g. a sweat-reducing t-shirt) can provide the extra comfort needed to make a journey more bearable.

Even with all these safety and comfort factors in place, however, there's absolutely no guarantee that I'll be able to continue, especially as my mind could go at any second. On-the-spot calming techniques such as stopping, closing your eyes, and re-centring for thirty seconds every so often really can help.

One gripe I have is that I wish I could just get up and down a mountain, enjoy the views, and have banter with my mates all the way, without any mental interference. My fear makes me slower, so I end up fading out of conversations as I try to battle my walking demons. Fortunately, my mates are cool and will often take it in shifts to stick with me, helping me move along. Having this connection is so important, and I really appreciate them putting up with my protestations and self-loathing.

The solutions I've mentioned above are what work for me personally, and I hope – if you have a fear of heights, or know somebody who wants to take on mountains but dreads them at the same time – that some of them will work for you too. However, the best advice I can give is this: if you don't feel you should risk it, don't. If you do want to do it, then gentle exposure therapy could provide a breakthrough.

Even with all the walks I've been on, I still become nervous and my palms still sweat whenever I watch mountain videos. Honestly, show me a photo of Everest and sometimes I have to remind myself it's just a photo! I look at those videos or I see other hikers when I'm on the mountains and I think, 'How can you be doing this and not be feeling nervous?' But, of course, I don't know what's going on in anybody else's mind. For all I know, they could have an inner voice screaming at them that the scale of the mission is too much or that taking on these heights is impossible. I don't know how much they may or may not have had to talk themselves up just to get to where they are that day. I've learnt that I can only focus on my own game plan – and that it will vary from hill to hill and mountain to mountain – for each peak is different and deserves respect.

It may not respect you – it neither loves nor hates, after all – but you must respect it.

Now, you might be asking why I didn't seek other means of help in order to conquer my fear of heights after we completed Scafell Pike, and the answer to that is simple: I didn't think of it! Looking back over the chapters of this book, it's clear to me that the obvious remedies often elude me, and may not present themselves for quite some time due to me not being the most practical person. In fact, it only struck me that I could look online to see what advice was available as I began writing this chapter! Remember what I said about being prepared as best as you can for hikes? Well, clearly I'm still learning.

My research has informed me that it's all about overcoming a very personal fear, as well as changing your mindset. Generally, people don't like to go out of their comfort zone, and when they eventually do venture outside of it, an exaggerated but very real fear can kick in. I mentioned that I have inner demons that bombard me whenever I'm on a mountain, and while other people's voices will be different, acknowledging those voices and the fear they represent is the first step to taking ownership of the problem and stepping foot on the path to conquering those fears.

I've mentioned exposure therapy, and it seems this is a shared view across a range of websites. Again, this relates to getting outside your comfort zone.

For most of us, going up mountains isn't exactly an everyday thing, and so constant exposure to a fear of mountain-related heights simply isn't possible. For those who live far away from mountains and have other life commitments, attempting to overcome a general fear of heights on a regular basis isn't always possible either.

As well as watching YouTube videos in order to prepare myself for future hikes, I also remind myself that I've taken on other mountains and achieved what I set out to do – something that encourages me to tackle the next one. I'm fortunate enough to live near several decent hills up to the 300-metre mark, which gives me some practice, and while you might think that's not high enough, walking up these hills repeatedly has definitely helped me deal with both the physical and mental aspects of taking on mountains.

From my own personal experience, I've found that another thing you can do to help you deal with a fear of heights is to keep a log of your journey up each mountain; reading back over it before you take on each new mountain will remind you of your achievements and of any coping strategies you'd previously developed. Also, when on a high altitude hike, I find using words like 'focus' and 'come on' can also help, especially when shouting them out loud. I'm never going to be somebody who can walk up a mountain in record-breaking time, but I know I can complete the walk when I really put my mind to it.

What I'm saying is, try to keep everything you've learnt as fresh in your mind as possible to help prepare you for next time. Search for online advice, look back at photos of previous hikes, and read testimonies of how others have conquered their fears. Any action is a positive action.

And, if it ever gets too much, slow down and take a breather. You may not have beaten any record times, but you will have beaten your fears and your own personal demons.

Other online advice appears to include Cognitive Behavioural Therapy, Virtual Reality training and meditation (see the 2020 chapter for my VR and meditation experiences), and paying a mountaineering instructor to assist you in overcoming your inner demons. There are even mountaineering courses tailored specifically for people with a fear of heights – though these may not be affordable to everybody.

From experience, I've found that being self-analytical and reflective is incredibly important. For instance, while on your walk, ask yourself the following questions: What is it particularly about being high up that causes you to melt down? How is thinking about it making you feel right now? What steps can you take in the next few seconds (as long as it doesn't endanger you) that will make the situation better? Are you in a position to turn around and go to a lower level place in order to keep your head clear? (For this last question, it's always important – if you do have to stop – to remember that you at least attempted it.)

Of course, these are just my own thoughts and reflections. Undoubtedly, if you're reading this and you suffer from any kind of fear of heights, then your phobia and the ways you deal with it may be different to mine. Either way, hopefully there's something you can pick up here.

Whether or not you have a fear of heights, this I know: once you've reached the top of a mountain and have returned to base level, the overwhelming sensation you gain on the completion of your mission can keep you buzzing for days.

That said, there will always be some who argue that if you don't make it to the top – if you have to give up at any point – then nothing has been gained. Well, I'm here to tell you, that point of view is wrong! I say you've turned up and attempted to take it on, and although it hasn't worked out this time, there's always the next time. You may find out, of course, that mountains aren't your thing, and that's okay too – there are plenty of other adventures to be had.

It's all in the preparation and, when you're ready, just pack your bag, stick on your shoes, and open your front door.

For more information on how to get over a fear of heights – or at least how to minimise the effects in order for you to continue your walk – see the 'Acrophobia Help' part of the Appendix.

Chapter Nineteen

TECHNOLOGY

While writing this book, I've embraced the idea that finding your own individual style in the world of hiking is important if you are to enjoy it. This is true from what you expect to get out of walks – whether your motivation be history, nature, geography, photography, or fitness – to the clothes you choose to wear and the equipment you choose to carry. It also applies to the level of technology you wish to use on your walks.

As you've probably gathered from this book, my utilisation of technology is not very complicated. I use my computer to research hikes from walking websites, or to create my own through Google Maps; the Street View option on Google Maps is a revelation for an airhead like me because it gives me the chance to recognise certain landmarks or roads when we're out and about. Using YouTube to check out areas I'll be visiting in advance has also helped me a lot.

All this may seem like it would take the spontaneity out of being in the Great Outdoors, but I've learnt that being prepared is incredibly important when it comes to reducing the chances of becoming lost – although it's certainly not foolproof – as well as (hopefully) reducing stress. It would be great to feel more free-spirited and to take these walks as I find them, but given my forgetfulness and fear of heights, I enjoy the walks more this way.

In the past – say, 20 to 30 years ago – hikers might have taken a camera, notepad and pen, maps, and guidebooks on their walks. Nowadays, however, a smartphone can replace any or all of those items – and it makes your backpack quite a bit lighter too. As long as there's decent reception, I've found that maps on smartphones work well (however, I will stress here yet again that having navigational skills and equipment is so important for hikes). The internet is useful when it comes to searching for walks, and for reading or watching how other people go about their hiking adventures, giving you instant info on history, geography, nature, and whatever else you're most interested in when it comes to your treks.

The only other bit of technology I use for my walking endeavours is a stepometer. It's extremely motivating to see the steps and distance increasing on a hike, or even when I'm just pootling about my hometown trying to hit 10,000 steps.

There are many phone apps you can use to map or track your walks. From speaking to family and friends about what apps they use for hikes, I've included a few in the Appendix to help you get started. However, please bear in mind that, as technology moves so fast, any advice I could give would soon be out of date. (Oh, okay, I'll make one quick recommendation: ViewRanger is what Robin uses, and this has been reliable in helping us keep on track on many of our adventures). The best thing to do is to search your app store to see what's available and then try some out to discover what works for you.

All this technology is great, but it can sometimes make my head spin, because all I really want to do when I'm in the countryside is to escape the hubbub of the city and enjoy the simplicity and beauty of where I'm at – to sit on a rock overlooking a valley, to wander past a babbling stream with birds chirping in the trees…it's the emotive experience that plays a part in drawing me to greener pastures. All this, plus – I get to eat a Cornish pasty in peace.

I'm not saying that technology takes away from the experience of being outside; when harnessed in the right way, and depending on your motivations, it can really add to the experience. Someone strolling along a hillside with a GPS, drone, digital camera, and stepometer may give the impression of a cyborg out for a walk, but if at least one of those devices is what draws them to the outdoors, then that's okay. Whoever they are, I just hope they'd occasionally leave their social media accounts unchecked or stop flying the drone for a moment to gain a deep sense of the world around them – though this takes a disciplined soul in the age of ultra-convenience.

Having said that, for anybody taking photos or using drones, there probably is a sense of them taking in the world around them as they scan the area for the wonders of beauty. The quest for a worthwhile snap is a noble one.

As is the quest for a Cornish pasty.

Chapter Twenty

HOW TO CHOOSE A WALK

If, after reading this book, you're ready to get out there but still aren't quite sure how to start, I've put together some ideas from my own experiences and research. I hope these assist you when starting your own walking endeavours.

One thing you can do is visit specialist walking websites, such as: www.mapmywalk.com and www.walkingbritain.com (just remember that the instructions you follow might be different – in some parts – to the walk you actually take, especially if the walk you're following is from a few years ago. At such times, it might be worth looking at a map of the area to see potential routes to the nearest town or village for a safe exit strategy).

Here are some other ideas:

Google search walks in your local area.
Download walking apps.
Work out your own route on Google Maps.
Buy walking guidebooks for your area – or further afield.
Buy a travel guidebook of Britain and use it to explore a certain city or town.

Study OS Maps at your local library or online – or even buy your own and head out with them.

Pick a random train station and go from there, seeing where you end up. No planning, just go for it.

Head out your front door, choose a direction to walk in, and see where that takes you for a couple of hours.

Visit YouTube or walking blog websites to develop your own ideas about how to create routes.

Turn up somewhere and use your phone to navigate (just make sure you have reception/internet/a full battery).

Visit hiking websites, where you can follow routes other people have already created.

Go on a hiking holiday.

Do a walking pilgrimage.

Plan a route with military efficiency, then deliberately get lost. Perhaps make this a common theme…no, hold on: that's just me. Please don't do this.

Walk round to family and/or friends' houses in your local area. I've done this before, calling on several people – either announced or unannounced – in one day. Just a quick two-minute-hello-call and then on to the next house. It's a sociable way to accumulate your daily steps.

Follow National Trust walks.

Explore local walking groups online, e.g. through meetup. com. Remember that there might be a small fee for each walk you take with such groups.

Pick a subject – e.g. history, geography, nature etc. – and use that as the main theme to research wherever you're walking. You can do your own DIY history or geography trail, for instance.

Try to reach your 10,000 steps by walking around your home and garden.

Join a Parkrun, but just walk it.

If possible, walk to work instead of driving or taking public transport. Or, walk halfway there and then take public transport. This might need a bit of planning and might require waking up earlier. You could also leave work early, walk part of the way, and then get the train/bus home from the next stop on.

Try playing Pokémon GO.

Go geocaching.

Relive your childhood – pretend you're fleeing from an evil monster's castle and that you won't be safe until you get to your target destination. Or, pretend you're a rebel working against the government, trying to get to a secret pick-up point to obtain a secret package that will aid your cause greatly. Set yourself a challenging – but realistic – time to do it in.

I've put together a suggested reading list of books I own that have inspired me to put my boots on in recent years. I hope this helps get you started on – or carry on with – your own adventures.

Conclusion

So, that's it – this brings us to the end of my little hiking book. I hope it's given you some ideas for walks, as well as some practical information, and – most importantly – the motivation to get out there and do it, no matter what physical or psychological things might be holding you back.

Personally, I'm so glad I decided to start hiking several years ago, and I hope to continue doing so for several more years to come – both for the mental and physical health benefits, and for the camaraderie I experience when taking on challenges with my friends.

I couldn't think of a better hobby to have, and remember: the longer you walk for, the more snacks you can have.

So, what are you waiting for? Get out there. Enjoy the fresh air. Enjoy the views. Enjoy all the other benefits you get from leaving your house and putting one foot in front of the other.

Be safe.

Walk.

Appendix

Useful Resources

All of these links are correct at the time of publication.

Accommodation: www.airbnb.co.uk

Date scheduling: www.agreeadate.com

Flight comparison sights: www.skyscanner.net and www. fly-scanner.com

Google Maps (UK): www.google.co.uk/maps

West Meon walk: http://fancyfreewalks.org/Hampshire/West-Meon.pdf?version=1702

Ben Nevis webcam: https://aboutfortwilliam.com/webcams/ben-nevis-and-fort-william

Ben Nevis website (1): https:www.visitscotland.com/see-do/iconic-scotland/ben-nevis

Ben Nevis website (2): www.walkinghighlands.co.uk/fortwilliam/bennevis.shtml

VR exposure therapy for acrophobia: https://ovrhealth.com/how-we-can-help/ and www.oasis-talk.org

Specialist walking websites: www.walkingbritain.com and www. mapmywalk.com

Suggestions for hiking apps from your smartphone's app store: Komoot; AllTrails; Map My Walk; ViewRanger.

Mindful Walking: The BUPA Podcast can be found at: https://www.bupa.co.uk/newsroom/ourviews/mindful-walking-meditation#:~:text=Mindful%20walking%20is%20a%20form,focus%20on%20the%20present%20moment.

A couple of videos for mindful walking include: https://youtu.be/xXYFNmFb6zY (from The Mindful Movement Channel) and https://youtu.be/8D3oh2Rdvyw (from the Great Meditation Channel). Or, just type the phrase 'walking meditation' into the YouTube search engine and take your pick of what's on offer.

Handy Tips

For exercise: Pop along to YouTube and tap 'workout videos' into the search bar. Change it up by putting in 'five-minute workouts' or '10-minute workouts', or just walk! Walking carries a myriad of benefits for both physical and mental health (see the chapter 'Why I Walk' for more information on how it's helped me).

For modern-day map reading: Whilst it's true that my paper map reading abilities are woefully limited – and while a lot of experienced hiking websites and books will tell you that such skills are essential in order to negotiate the countryside and mountainous areas – I've found that plotting walks using Google Maps can be fun. I also like to use the Street View options for certain sections of walks, as it gives me an idea of any surrounding landmarks I can look to in case we get lost. The only drawback is that it may take away the surprise of seeing a monument or stately home, say, for the first time. I'd even go as far as to say there's a certain joy in creating DIY routes, as it gives the whole walk a real personal element.

For walking in the city: Buy a guidebook on Britain, pick a town or city, then head out and explore. Design your own day out by doing an internet search for locations of interest, then plan the transport links to each one – or just walk to them. Use Tripadvisor to search locations and places of interest. Turn up in a big city or town without a plan and just see where the day takes you.

For Virtual Walks: Whilst it would be laborious to list every country and video suggestion for each, here I offer a few ideas to get you started on your world tour. In the YouTube search bar, type in the phrase 'Virtual Hike/Walk' followed by a country name, and see where it takes you. If you're interested in finding out more about certain countries, then do a bit of research to see which monuments, museums and parks there are in that particular country and look to see if there are any tours of those. To get you started, try searching 'British Museum Virtual Tour' or 'Vatican Virtual Tour'.

It's fair to say that some countries are better represented than others when it comes to virtual tours and hikes. if you find this to be the case, then try watching a documentary about a country on YouTube instead. For some countries you might find official tourist videos as well. Alternatively, you'll more than likely find a YouTuber who's put up a video of their visit to your chosen country (it's fair to say that some of these videos may not be of the best quality, though, and really quite short). The best YouTubers for doing a world tour from home include Drew Binsky and Gabriel Traveler.

Virtual Cycling: Similar advice applies to searching for cycling tours on YouTube: just pop in 'Virtual Cycling Tour' and the country of your choice into the search bar. At the time of writing, I'm not sure if all countries are represented. I just searched for 'Cycling Tour Of The World' and it seems that there are a plethora of YouTubers documenting their travels for you to cycle along with. Also, even though I don't own a motorbike, there's a community of YouTubers that have documented their travels on their bikes. For this, I can recommend the Itchy Boots channel to cycle along to in order to get you started.

Cooking: If you're interested in cooking outside, I'd recommend you start with a camping gas stove set-up. I've included some info in this Appendix on a cheap basic set-up to help get you started. Building fires is a particular skill and should only be attempted by an experienced hand in a safe environment, away from others. Two YouTubers who do outdoor fireside cooking and who I like watching are Kent Survival and Simon, A Bloke In The Woods.

Acrophobia Help

Some people might not know they have a fear of heights until they start walking up mountains, in which case it's a good idea to be aware of the symptoms of acrophobia. Physical symptoms can include:

Profuse sweating, chest pain or tightness, and an increased heart rate at the sight or thought of high places.

Shaking, nausea, light-headedness, and vomiting when faced with or thinking about heights.

A sensation of dizziness or a loss of balance when you look up at a high place or when you look down from a height.

Avoiding heights in daily life.

Psychological symptoms can include:

Fear of being trapped somewhere high up.

Panicking when performing or thinking about performing any action that involves heights. This may even include going upstairs or looking up at/down from a multi-storey building.

Experiencing excessive distress at the thought of encountering heights in the future.

If you do have a fear of heights, the good news is there are plenty of ways you can deal with your phobia, some of which I'm going to list here. Personally, I've tried many of these things and can recommend them, whereas with others (such as CBT and counselling) I haven't done them myself but have heard great things from people who have. If you're interested in any of these, a quick Google search will bring up all kinds of useful information. So, here are some of the things you can try when overcoming a fear of heights:

Practice meditation techniques. Pop along to YouTube and type in the search bar a phrase such as 'Five-minute meditation' or '10-minute mediation'. More specifically, typing in 'Acrophobia Meditation' brings up several options as well. As with any of the above, please consult your GP/relevant specialist before undertaking meditation as a treatment option.

Visualise the hill or mountain and imagine yourself striding up it. Immerse yourself in the surroundings and the sounds, and use your imagination to conjure up what you can feel and smell. Watching YouTube videos or looking at pictures of the hill/mountain you intend to conquer may assist with this.

Enter phrases such as 'mountain walking with acrophobia' or 'mountain walking fear of heights' into a search engine to access articles and guidance that may provide you with the knowledge required to deal with your issues.

Keep a journal of each hill you hike to inspire you to take on new feats. This may help you keep track of what works and what doesn't work for you (and when).

Have a discussion with your hiking partner about how you feel and how they may be able to assist you during the hike.

Seek out a fully-trained mountain guide who will offer you the best support on the day of the trek. Typing the name of the mountain/area you intend to visit plus the phrase 'mountaineering guide' should bring up some options.

Visit a discussion forum such as www.walkingforum.co.uk to gain advice on all kinds of walking-related matters.

Undertake a mountain adventure course that deals with tackling your fear of heights (if it's within your budget). One website to get you started is www.will4adventure. com. Once you've completed the main course, they offer follow-up sessions too.

Seek a counselling service that deals with phobias. Ask about Cognitive Behavioural Therapy, which may challenge and reframe your negative thoughts about heights. A counsellor can be arranged privately or via your GP.

Some counselling services now offer a route to Virtual Reality exposure therapy for acrophobia. You might need to search what services are local to you, and a counsellor or your GP may be able to assist with this. Look at the resources section in this Appendix for some helpful links.

Apps have also been developed for use at home with VR headsets, but it would be best to take advice from a health professional before pursuing this approach. Ideas of apps to use include Acrophobia VR, ZeroPhobia – Fear Of Heights, and VR Heights Phobia. At the time of writing, smartphone-friendly VR headsets can be purchased from about £7.99 upwards on Amazon. Please refer to the 2020 chapter for my experiences with VR. Again, it is advisable to undertake advice from a GP before starting home VR sessions.

It may be that a referral to a psychiatrist is needed in order to overcome a debilitating fear of heights.

When you're out and about on a hill:

Practice: Do a few low-level hills first. Then, if you feel okay, build up to the next height level. The more you put yourself in a situation involving heights, the more manageable it will hopefully become for you.

When you're high up, acknowledge that there will most likely be some level of fear involved. Hopefully, all the preparation work you do beforehand will help you to rationalise your anxiety.

Try using hiking poles.

Take a break to steady yourself. Mediate, take deep breaths, suck a sweet, or chat to a friend…anything that helps you calm down and carry on.

Slow down if you have to.

Try to avoid looking down (though this is easier said than done, especially if you're on the way back down a mountain).

Break the journey down into sections. If there's a rocky outcrop 30 metres ahead, aim for that. Then, if there's a bend in the path another 40 metres ahead, aim for that. And so on.

If you'd feel safer crawling along certain sections, then do so.

If you have to stop completely, there's no shame in that. The hill or mountain will still be there, waiting for you, another time. Or, if you chose not to try it again, just remember that there are plenty of other walks to be had.

Further Reading For Tackling Your Fear Of Heights

www.miramonticorteno.com – 'How to get rid of your fear of heights when hiking'.

www.explore-share.com – 'Mountaineering: How to Overcome Fear of Heights'.

www.bmc.co.uk – 'Aim High: Four Tips To Fight Your Fear of Heights'.

www.walkingforum.co.uk – this website is a discussion place for all walking-related topics. Just look for advice dealing with heights, acrophobia and vertigo.

www.psycom.net – 'Acrophobia (The Fear Of Heights): Are You Acrophobic?'

www.anxietyuk.org.uk – 'Heightened Anxiety: How To Overcome A Fear Of High Places'.

Further Reading To Inspire You To Do Your Own Walks

Strumpshaw, Tincleton and Giggleswick's Joyously Busy Great British Adventure Map (www.marvellousmaps.com)

Engel's England by Matthew Engel

Microadventures by Alastair Humphreys

The Bluffer's Guide To Hiking by Simon Whaley

Extreme Sleeps by Phoebe Smith

100 Outstanding British Walks by Ordnance Survey

Lundy, Rockall, Dogger, Fair Isle by Mathew Clayton and Anthony Atkinson

Tiny Britain by Dixe Wills

DK Eyewitness Travel: Great Britain with main contributor Michael Leapman

Travel Stories and Highlights: 2019 Edition edited by Robert Fear

Islandeering: Adventures Around The Edge Of Britain's Hidden Islands by Lisa Drewe

The Peak Bagging Log Book: County Tops Of The United Kingdom by Matthew Arnold

Contact

Thanks for buying and reading this book. It means a lot to me.

If you'd like to know more about any aspect of this book, get further advice on hiking, or just let me know what you think about my work, you can email me at: waynewrites100@outlook.com

My website can be found at: www.waynemullane.wordpress.com – here you'll find updates on my hiking adventures as well as my short stories and poems. You can connect with me there too by leaving a comment at the end of any article.

It'd be great to hear from you ☺.

Acknowledgements

A big shout out to JJ, Mum, Dad, and my whole family for all your support as I wrote this book. You were all there to listen to what I'd written or to pull me through when the end didn't quite seem in sight. Writing this book has been an adventure in itself and I'm so glad you were all part of it.

To my friends Robin, Robert, Aaron and Pete – this book would not have been possible without the adventures we've been on. Thanks for all the memories and banter along the way. Here's looking forward to future excursions in a post-pandemic world.

To Jessica Grace Coleman of Coleman Editing for the high-quality proofreading, editing and constant support. When I was lost as to how to carry on with the book when the pandemic hit, I'll always remember how your advice steadied and spurred me on to get this book completed.

Big thanks to Leila and Dan for all your support, as always.

To Laura Antonioli for the wonderful cover design and typesetting. I'll always appreciate your commitment to completing the work and supporting me with the last minute changes.

To my Welsh brethren: love and respect, as always.

To my work colleagues - Cheers Team Awesome Force.

Massive thank you to Hollie Marsh for the constant support to get the book onto Kindle and with the marketing side of things. Your guidance, navigation and patience has provided me with invaluable lessons on my self-publishing journey.

Printed in Great Britain
by Amazon

75131899R00123